Winning In The Workplace

Also By John C. LaBella

<u>The Inside Of Outsourcing</u>
- A Pragmatic View From The Inside

Winning In The Workplace

John C. LaBella

Copyright © 2014 By John C. LaBella,

All rights reserved.

Published in the United States by LCI,
an imprint of LCI Publishing Group.
Madison, Wisconsin.

ISBN   978-0-9855536-4-7

Printed in the United States of America MMXIV.

Cover design and graphics by:
Kurt B. Schoenfielder, Throttle 5 Design
www.Throttle5.com

About the Author

John C. LaBella spent more than 25 years helping firms optimize their core processes. In this book, <u>Winning In The Workplace</u>, John focuses on the relationships and behaviors of people working within these processes. His advice on how to succeed in the workplace is of value to anyone starting a career or wishing to rejuvenate one.

John's managerial experience spans manufacturing, logistics and the IT function. During his tenure at Kraft Foods Inc. he led the team responsible for creating the manufacturing and distribution processes for Lunchables©, and other innovative product lines. John also created the strategic roadmap for supply chain applications and managed the offshoring of application support services for the global IT group.

At Gap, Inc., John managed their groundbreaking journey from staff augmentation to a managed services model in their IT department. In less than six months, all application support activities migrated to a new outsourcing partner. His outsourcing experience led to his first book, <u>The Inside of Outsourcing</u>. This is a practical "must read" for executives. It is also a practitioner's guide through the varied activities resulting in successful outsourcing experiences.

John has traveled the globe working with partners in the U.S., Canada, Mexico, Brazil, Eastern Europe, Western Europe and India. John taught Operations Management at the University of Wisconsin, Madison - School of Business and at Edgewood College in the MBA program. John was invited to lecture at L'Université de Bordeaux in Bordeaux, France and also at the Massachusetts Institute of Technology, Cambridge, MA.

Acknowledgments:

I would be remiss if I didn't take a moment to thank the various teams and leaders I have been fortunate to work with over the years. Without their encouragement along the way, this book would be nothing but empty pages.

During my career, each has offered ideas, support and a unique opportunity to help me understand how to "*Win in the Workplace.*"

I would also like to thank my wife Patti, Darlene Kozarek and Patti Gutowski for helping me develop content and edit my numerous deviations from accepted grammatical norms.

A special thanks goes to my burger-buddy John. His honest feedback on a range of topics was invaluable and kept me focused on the topic.

For the "Bigs", AJ and Cooper,
the "Middles", Bella and Ryan,
and the "Littles", Adeline and Carter.
Your imagination and enthusiasm for life
inspires me every day.

"Winning isn't everything, it's the only thing!"

"The dictionary is the only place that success comes before work. Hard work is the price we must pay for success. I think you can accomplish anything if you're willing to pay the price."

"The achievements of an organization are the results of the combined effort of each individual."

Vincent "Vince" Lombardi (1913-1970)

Table of Contents

Forward

1. **Understanding Workplace Politics**   page 1
   Everyone reports to someone
   Learn how to manage up
   What's really going on
   How are you perceived
   Respect the job – and the fact that you have one

2. **Communicating Effectively**   page 15
   How you say what you say counts
   Keeping Cool
   What you say can (and usually will) be held against you
   Knowledge is power

3. **Organizational Structure**   page 27
   The shape of the organization
   Span of control – Narrow, Wide, Optimal
   Designed for internal efficiencies
   Why are bosses needed

4. **Managing Your Job**   page 39
   What is a job anyway
   Every job is part of an overarching process
   Improving process throughput
   Understanding your point of difference
   Manage your time wisely
   Are you bored doing the same job day after day

5. **Managing Paradigms**   page 55
   What is a paradigm
   Paradigm paralysis
   Recognizing and managing a paradigm shift

6. **Selling and Negotiating**   page 63
   Selling wreaths during the Holidays
   There is only one solution to any problem – yours
   Support ideas with facts and data…avoid saying "I think"
   Negotiating
   Know when to hold 'em, and know when to fold 'em
   The next one that talks loses

7. **Managing Others**   page 77
   Managing people
   What is the role of your team
   Set goals, secure resources, and get out of the way
   Managing with Statistical Process Control
   Things managers should not do
   Things managers should do more of

8. **Managing Projects**   page 93
   The five essential steps of project management
   Problem definition
   Plan the work
   Work the plan
   Monitor progress
   Project closeout

9. **Leading and Leadership**   page 105
   What is leadership
   Follow the leader
   The role of leadership
   Learning to lead
   Can a person lead and manage at the same time
   Can an organization exist without leadership

10. **Managing Your Career**   page 117
    Where are you headed (career-wise)
    Managing your career path
    Jobs are both specific tasks and experiential opportunities
    Reading the signs – is a "course change" needed
    Preparing for your next career move
    The moment of truth – pursuing a job change

Closing   page 135

Forward:

"Winning In The Workplace"

The premise for this book is that for the most part, new hires in the workplace have yet to develop the "*soft skills*" they will need to succeed. Hiring decisions are often based on readily available data such as one's grade point average and extra curricular activities. The typical resume tells the hiring manager *what* you have done, but not *how* you did it. *How* you do what you do is the difference between long-term success and failure. New hires are left with the challenge of developing office acumen, interpersonal skills and leadership abilities on their own after they are hired. This book will help accelerate the learning process.

During my years in Corporate America and Academia, I have worked with many outstanding individuals. There were also those that didn't have a clue about how to work with others. Their salty personalities made it difficult for them to engage with subordinates, peers, and most importantly, their bosses. By sharing observations from my own experiences, the reader will develop ways to improve his or her soft skills, tactics and ability to navigate through office politics. The book is written from a universal perspective allowing the advice contained herein to be helpful to anyone in any profession.

The evidence supports the notion that a college education is an important element for future success. According to a 2004 Spencer Stuart survey, 97% of the CEO's from the S&P 500 firms have a college degree; 30% of those have MBS's. Sure, there are a number of examples of successful individuals that did not earn a college degree: Jobs, Gates, Zuckerberg, Ellison and Dell to name a few. These five are key to the success of Apple, Microsoft, Facebook, Oracle, and Dell Computers, building them to a combined market value that exceeds one trillion dollars. Statistically they are an anomaly. However, we can learn from anomalies by understanding why they are outliers in the first place. What are the traits and behaviors that set these five apart from the millions of others without degrees, working hard to eke out a living income?

Education is great, but some skills required in the boardroom that are not taught in school include:

- Understanding how to master the power of office politics.

- Creating a vision that inspires others.

- Effective communication – how to say what you say.

- Selling your ideas and selling yourself.

If not in college, where do leaders learn how to succeed? Parents can make a difference by helping their children develop the soft skills academia is not able to teach. For example:

- Teaching children to take pride in achieving goals through hard work and creativity, rather than being rewarded for simply showing up or being naturally smart.

- Providing opportunities to interact with others through play such as effectively using building blocks, sharing the paper and negotiating which crayon to use.

- Teaching them to be empathetic to the needs of others and demonstrate how to get involved with actions that "scratch the itch," instead of standing by wallowing in guilt.

- Giving them opportunities to lead others.

Landing that first job is top of mind for college graduates and of course, their parents. Higher education is a great place to learn about the technical aspects of certain job activities and processes. A wealth of knowledge, often in narrow fields of study, is passed on to the student. Unfortunately, and with few exceptions, success in the workplace often involves more than simply performing job activities well. Winning in the workplace requires social interactions across many functions. Doing this well is as important as doing your job properly.

- *Those unable to relate to others will watch their careers fizzle.* The book will identify skills, relationships and attitudes needed to keep one's job and enable success.

- *Success is not attained by random chance.* It is a result of being able to manage processes and lead others. The book will discuss at length the difference between managing and leading. Doing both of these well will enhance your ability to win in the workplace. Those that fail at these will simply start at the bottom and move over.

- *Success is defined by what people think you do rather than what you actually do.* The production of an output is the essence of work. How that product is valued depends on how it is marketed. Marketing your success in the workplace starts by building a set of positive perceptions about yourself.

Believe me, I have flaws. My own career history is filled with ups and downs, successes and failures. I have personally exhibited actions and attitudes that can quickly derail a career or, at the very least, keep it from rising quickly. Fortunately, I learned to adapt and adopt positive attributes. In so doing, I have been fortunate to accumulate enough wealth to retire in my 50's and maintain a comfortable lifestyle.

The old adage, "only the strong survive" should be supplanted by the notion that survival belongs to those that are able to adapt.

Please enjoy reading, *"Winning in the Workplace."*

Chapter 1: Understanding Workplace Politics

<u>Everyone reports to someone!</u>

Perhaps you decided to read this book because you are having issues with your job, your career or your boss. Some people are concerned about all three! Digging beneath the surface, the predominant issue usually involves one's boss. We all report to someone. Even self-employed entrepreneurs, who may not have a boss per se, need to maintain a *"boss-like"* relationship with their customers. The boss (or customer) is the gatekeeper to one's success. I learned that the hard way.

Shortly after graduating from college, I took a job as a third shift sanitation supervisor. The pay was good but the hours were hard to get used to. After 6 months on third shift, I was moved to second shift as a production supervisor. The boss was difficult to work for. I hated the job, and the hours kept me away from the family. I especially hated the *"suits"* that were all heading home as I was arriving for work. I dressed like a slob, the F-word dominated my vocabulary and I would shower every 3 or 4 days whether I needed one or not. I had no desire to become one of the *"suits"* and vowed I would do everything in my power to work against the establishment.

Maybe it was the times. In the early 1970's everyone was anti-establishment and I was no exception. The lingering smell of tear gas and National Guard troops on campus during anti-Vietnam War riots were still fresh in my mind. The *"suits"* were part of the establishment and I was not going to conform and become one of them. This attitude permeated my psyche for a few years. I was not good at office politics but I was good at making observations. I noticed that the more I fought the establishment, the more difficult it became for me to succeed at my job.

During my anti-establishment years, it was myself against the world, and by God, I was going to win. Unfortunately, I observed that the *"suits"* knew how to conform to play the game, and conforming helped *them* win the game. They were smooth and got along with everyone. They never had a negative thing to say especially about their bosses. In fact, they were very good at what I called, *"kissing up."* They had nice cars, comfortable homes, and better pay than I did. Still, the thought of *"kissing up"* made me want to gag. Then I noticed something else; the bosses took care of the *"suits."* They backed them in meetings, defended them to others, and promoted them. What was happening?

A symbiotic relationship? The kiss-ups benefited by kissing up. How did the boss benefit? Perhaps it was ego stroking, perhaps something else. The two *"species"* (boss and kiss-up) existed to serve each other. Maybe, just maybe, the *"suits"* had figured something out, something very valuable. They found that a positive relationship with the boss would yield many rewards. I decided that I wanted those same rewards for my family. I wanted my kids to have nice vacations; live comfortably; and attend quality schools.

I realized the boss was the one person that held the power to help me achieve my goals or stand in the way. My *"Ah Hah"* moment came when I finally realized my boss was the most important person in my job life. It took me about fifteen years to figure this out. Once I did, the work-world changed for me. The sooner you realize this, the better. Hopefully, with the help of this book, you can be a little smarter than I was.

In most cases the boss works for the same company you do, however, the boss may also be that buyer you are trying to sell something to. Think broadly; think symbiotic – I'll scratch your back if you scratch mine.

You will rarely, if ever, win a confrontation with your boss. Your boss didn't just fall off the turnip truck last week. Even though you may find it hard to believe, someone trusted his or her abilities to manage a team and promoted your boss into that position. Since no one ever wants to admit they made a bad hire or promotion decision, the boss's boss is going to take sides too. They will usually defend their decision and back your boss. When you decide to fight the boss you are also fighting those above the boss. You are in a no-win situation. If you *are* able to "beat the boss" no one else, especially the boss's boss, will want you working for them for fear that someday you will also take them on. Fighting workplace politics quickly poisons your career. This is true even if you win in the courts or become a whistleblower.

I am not saying every boss is great and *you* are the one with the problem. The truth is that many bosses are unqualified to be in the position they are in. I have worked for some real clinkers too. Just remember, regardless of how bad that boss is, when you fight the boss you are creating a new problem, (namely you) that will need to be dealt with and believe me, you will be. Don't expect a direct confrontation at the bike racks after work. Office politics will begin discrediting you in subtle ways. Here is what to watch for. For fear of legal repercussions, most people will never discuss the actual case with you directly. People will begin to question your credentials, work output, and character. The boss and others will ostracize you and stop confiding in you. This means they don't trust you! Soon the work environment becomes unfriendly, perhaps even hostile, and you will seek other employment. Be very careful explaining why you left when you talk to your future employer. If you still want to take on the boss, remember this: The stakes are very high so think it through very carefully as *you* have everything to lose!

Sorry Charlie, there are not many options for you when you get stuck working for a bad boss. Going to HR is risky at best. It is hard to determine how they will react. Will they support you or the boss? Nothing, and I mean NOTHING you share with anyone about your boss will be held in confidence. Protection for whiners and whistleblowers is somewhat of a myth contrived by those in power to expose the moles in the organization. Your boss is part of the power structure in the organization. The political clout he or she has will end up demonizing and discrediting you. It effectively convinces people to believe that *YOU* are the problem.

About the best you can hope for when working for a bad boss is the patience to wait until you or your boss gets moved to a different position. Of course, you can always quit, and find a different job somewhere else. Unfortunately, they usually ask for references. If you have a bad relationship with your boss, you probably shouldn't include her as a reference. When your most recent boss is not listed as a reference, all sorts of red flags go up. So what, you may ask, should you do?

<u>Learn how to manage up:</u>

In addition to doing your job well, you need to learn how to keep your boss happily supporting your career. This is called *"managing up."* It is the most effective way to create and maintain a positive relationship with your boss and other persons in authority. Projecting a positive, productive image will bode well for you when decisions are made concerning promotions or the *"right sizing"* (i.e. layoffs) of staff. If you want to learn how to manage up, consider the following.

- *Be punctual!* For crying out loud, do I need to tell you this? Your parents have probably tried to beat this into you for years and for good reason. Being on time every day may not earn you any extra points. However, being late all the time will eventually land you in the doghouse. Unless you happen to be a *"charity-hire"* (i.e. your parents know the manager or your uncle owns the company or something like that) you are expected to contribute. Being at the office and visible shows folks that you are dedicated and that you have a work ethic that builds trust and reliability. Of all the things you control, being punctual is at the top of the list. Don't blow it!! It is possible to be a well-liked, productive worker, yet still end up fired for being repeatedly tardy. Take note – you are replaceable!

- *Pay attention in meetings.* When you attend meetings with your boss or other managers, you need to spend a whole lot more time listening than talking. You will learn that managers like to ramble on at times as it makes them feel important. You need to devote full attention to what is going on in order to understand the message. This means NO checking your phone messages, email, texting, etc. This is most critical when you are new and have yet to learn the lingo every company uses. Your job is to understand the basic essence of the message presented in the meeting, not to fight it! Be careful not to interrupt the boss, no matter how important your comments may be.

Ask good questions. It is ok to ask a few questions during meetings, when appropriate, to clarify points. Never, ever ask the type of question that could put someone on the spot in a public setting, especially your boss. A good question can be self-rewarding, even if you do not get good answers. By asking well thought, probing (but not accusatory) questions you show an interest in or a grasp of the subject. This can be flattering to the presenter. Good questions not only show one's understanding of the topic, they also help others reach a better understanding. As a manager, I enjoyed good questions and discussion during or after my presentations. I used this feedback to make revisions to the presentation and sometimes to my personal philosophy as well. I generally felt that if the audience didn't get it, I did a poor job presenting it. Try rephrasing your manager's concern back to her and ask if you understood it correctly. Of course, you need to be careful not to ask a question already answered. That's a sure sign you were sleeping, daydreaming or texting someone during the presentation and that's a no-no.

- *Keep your manager in the loop.* Managers hate *"getting caught stupid"* or unaware of something critical happening in the group. I am not an advocate of *"managing-by-minutia."*

This is when your boss needs to know every nicky-ticky detail for fear of *"getting caught stupid."* Every team faces issues on a daily basis. Many of these can (and should) be resolved as they arise, by the people on the team. That is why we have teams and precisely what they are being paid to do.

- *Tell me about stuff that you can't resolve.* I never asked my people to issue routine written postings. By the time they are written, circulated and read, the information is well out of date. I did want to know about issues that were unable to be resolved within the defined service level agreement (SLA). These are important, especially if they create issues for other processes that may raise complaints to my manager. We will cover SLA's in more detail later.

  The leader of any group needs to be aware of the critical issues. My general definition of "critical" is an unresolved incident that could result in missing a goal; cause havoc on some other part of the firm; creates financial risk or impacts customers. I wanted to know about these. You should seek feedback from your manager to learn what it is they want to know about. Ask how often he or she wants to hear from you and in what format. Remember what I said about written postings? That's me! Your manager may have a totally different perspective.

- *Be clear in meetings.* Brainstorming is fine, but not in every meeting. We will cover how to present yourself and your ideas in more detail later in the book. For now, remember to sit down and plan your thoughts in advance. Try to be clean, clear, and quick. These are good skills to hone. I had the pleasure of working for a boss that presented three clear points to bolster his thoughts. It was his trademark. Every time he did a presentation he shared his three key points. It is ok if your points are not always of a complimentary nature. If you do offer criticism, be respectful. Cite facts and stay away from personal attacks. (Does this really need to be said?) If you take the time to follow critiques and complaints with proposed solutions, you will be seen as a problem-solver, not a complainer.

- *Tell your manager what you need.* Be careful not to become overwhelmed by saying, *"yes"* to every request. Don't assume your manager understands all of the tasks on your plate. When your plate is full, learn to say, "I will be happy to take on this new request but I am also working on these other projects, so how should I prioritize them?" Asking for help prioritizing gives a positive message to your boss. It says you want to do all you can but simply only have so many hours in the day.

- *More than the nature of the problem itself, your attitude will determine its outcome.* It is very likely your boss manages a team of people, making it important for you learn how to get along with your colleagues. Infighting creates friction, can be detrimental to team results and makes life harder for the boss. Be helpful, respectful, and polite. For crying out loud, don't gossip. Maintain a positive "can do" attitude at all times even when it is a challenge for you. Often, it is not the most talented that rise to the top, but those whom people actually like working with.

- *It's not a democracy, get over it!* Your boss has the final word on any decision. That's just the way it is. Our job as subordinates is to make sure the boss is aware of the important aspects and alternatives that are germane to making the best decision. We can try to influence the decision but ultimately, it is the boss's call. The boss is a critical link between you and the strategic mission that comes from the boss's boss. The primary role of your boss is not to babysit you but to keep you, and the rest of the team, aligned and supporting the overarching goals of the organization. Sometimes you may not understand (or be privy to) how your actions link into the bigger picture. It is fine to point out concerns along the way but in the final analysis, your boss makes the call.

What's really going on?

Reading between the lines in meetings. I can't tell you how many meetings I've attended in which the discussion had little to do with the posted agenda. My observations have been boiled down to four primary reasons that explain why people either host or attend meetings.

1. *Changing direction.* Someone wants the organization to agree to move forward with a new idea. Although a very common reason to meet, it may not be obviously stated on the agenda. Office politics being what they are, new ideas are often "pre-sold" to the various stakeholders before hand. The meeting ends up being window dressing.

2. *Protecting turf.* Issues have multiple perspectives. It is likely that someone attending the meeting will not like the new idea. Their intent is to offer a different direction or perhaps stop the recommendation cold. This will be done subtly and show great political acumen.

3. *Status updates.* Information sharing across a large segment of the organization is another reason to meet. This is a broad category and includes the status of important goals, updates on a specific projects and milestones achieved. I would consider training sessions to also be an information sharing type of meeting.

4. *The donuts!* Sad but true, the meetings with the highest level of attendance usually offer food and refreshments. To my delight, I found this was a global phenomenon and one that I personally enjoyed! Whether it was those luscious little puff pastries in Brazil, a full breakfast in India or beignets in New Orleans, it was all very good!

It is not unusual to find all four under-currents flowing through the same meeting, especially points one and two. The next time you go to a meeting, try to figure out who is attending the meeting and for what reason.

Status updates are rather tame events. Irrefutable facts (or factoids which are the illusion of fact without all the calories) are presented and should be reliable. Of course there are times when the facts are shaded or slanted in a particular direction. This disguises the truth for political reasons such as maintaining employment or the desire to *"stay the course"* on a project. Over time, the experience you gain will help you see through these boardroom ruses more clearly.

Direction changing meetings can be very interesting to watch. Try to figure out which side of the issue each member is on. You should watch and take a lesson about being politically savvy from these folks. The players will remain civil and non-confrontational. However, there were a few times I thought the sides were close to blows when they couldn't agree.

Meetings are the venue where modern-day turf battles are fought and won. Those that win do so without being overly obnoxious. They present a compelling reason to change, such as the *"burning platform"* analogy, "We need to act now or face the fire." They will present a fact-based case and let folks digest it rather than forcing it down their throats. It may actually take a few meetings to get people on board with the change. They will also identify the risks and unknowns the change may generate, while offering plans to mitigate them. This is a skillful move on the presenter's part and will tend to defuse the arguments from the opposition.

Those opposing the change won't be jumping up and down and beating on the table. They will ask skillfully constructed questions that act to create doubt and concern among the decision makers. They may look like they are supporting the change, even though they are not. Once you understand the position and perspective of each key stakeholder, things will really start to make sense to you. When it is your turn to host a meeting, you will have developed the skills to anticipate questions and where resistance may come from. We will go into more detail about how to construct *"selling points"* for your meetings in a later chapter.

How are you perceived?

Dress for success. Every job site has rules about acceptable dress and behavior. When they are written and posted for all to see there should be no excuse for violations. However, there are office settings in which many (if not all) of the rules are not posted. Don't make the mistake of thinking they don't exist, they are simply not posted. Where the rules are not posted, the new team member will need to learn proper behavior by observing and following others. It is wise to error on the side of being more conservative rather than less. Naturally there will be a range of behaviors across any group of people spanning the gamut from outrageous to a bit more conservative. For example, most of the team will wear clothing that covers the midriff but there will be that one guy or gal that wants to show off their artfully pierced naval. Although most of the staff wears pants that are classified as *"business casual"* there will be that leggy blond wearing short shorts. I'm not opposed to leggy blonds or short shorts, but there is a time and a place. In the office, during work hours, is neither the time nor place. Use common sense when you dress for work and think about this: would your mother approve or would she whack you upside the head with a 2x4? When it comes to dress and behavior, you will do yourself a favor by playing it more on the conservative side.

Workplace romances. Let me take a moment to talk about romantic relationships in the office. My mother has a saying that was passed down from her Sicilian grandmother *"non merda dove si mangia"* which loosely translates to "don't mess where you eat." In other words, and I know it is a rough translation, don't engage in work-place encounters of the romantic kind. They usually end badly and may result in one party or the other getting fired.

Working side-by-side with your current (or ex) lover creates a passel of social issues. The worst situation of all is a boss-subordinate relationship. Co-workers will be uncomfortable confiding in their teammates out of fear that things may get back to the boss. They will be convinced that little Jimmy or Joanie received special treatment, a promotion or a better raise, not because they deserved it but because of their special relationship with the boss. For these reasons, it is not unusual for the subordinate to be shunned and ostracized by the rest of the workgroup until they eventually leave. The bosses will fair better than the subordinates but they too will lose the respect and support of the rest of the team. The best advice is to keep romantic encounters out of the office all together. That said, I realize that once you leave school, the workplace may be one of the few places where you can meet other singles. If you must date people where you work, keep the lovey-dovey stuff low key in the office and for Pete's sake, don't get involved with someone in the same chain of command. You are there to work, not play.

Fitting into the culture. One of the common concerns I hear is "I just don't fit into the culture" or "I feel like the office outcast." This is pretty common for anyone joining a new workgroup regardless of whether you are in the mailroom or at the V.P. level. The existing peer group has history together. They have achieved success together and worst of all, they have created a paradigm in which they are quite comfortable. Now they are expected to open their arms and work with some *"wet-behind-the-ears"* newbie who has neither won their respect nor trust. If you are that newbie trying to fit in, eventually you will. Do your job in a respectful, non-threatening way, and soon you will be laughing it up with the rest of the gang at the water cooler. It may take a little time to win the trust of your co-workers but stick with it. The cliques tend to be strongest in teams that have not experienced a lot of turnover. You can expect to be the newbie until the next new person is hired, so enjoy it while you can.

On the other hand, you may never be accepted, especially if you bring the threat of radical change to the status quo. Organizations are good at creating paradigms. A paradigm is the accepted way of thinking about and understanding the way things work. A paradigm shift represents a new or unique way of viewing the world and for many, a threat to their comfort zone. We will examine paradigms more deeply in a later chapter. For now, understand that *"paradigm pioneers,"* a term coined by Joel Barker, live on the edge and are rarely embraced by their peers. They exist to enact, manage and generate change within the workplace. During my career I have held a number of positions in which my role was to *"break the mold."* I was hired to change paradigms and thereby affect the comfort zones of my peers. It took a long time for me to be accepted. In some cases I never was.

Respect the job – and the fact that you have one!

Stick to the rules. Remember the rules we discussed about acceptable attire and behavior? Well, there are also rules regarding attendance, tardiness, sick days, time off, etc. Do you really need to be lead by the nose through this stuff? You are being paid real money in exchange for performing a real task or job. Work rules provide a structured environment in which that task is to be performed. If you don't like the rules, leave. Don't expect the owner of the business or his representative, your boss, to change things just for you. That is not to say you shouldn't point things out and question (in a nice way) what doesn't make sense to you. Sometimes rules were created for reasons that are not readily apparent and/or just not pertinent any more.

I heard a story once about preparations for a large family feast. The lady of the house was in charge of preparing a ham. In so doing, she took a meat saw out of the drawer and cut off about 2 inches of the shank end and threw it away. She was asked why she did that and answered, "Because her mother always did it." When her mother was asked why she did it, surprisingly, she gave the same answer, "Because my mother did it." Fortunately, Grandma was there and when asked why she cut the shank end off and threw it away, she said, with a twinkle in her eye, "Because the pan was too small." The ham, by the way, was great although cutting the shank end off had nothing to do with it. Often, habits linger for no good reason.

Managing perceptions. A perception is defined as organization, identification, and interpretation of sensory information. They are used to represent and understand the environment and the people in that environment. As it pertains to this book, perceptions are how others view you. That may either be good or bad. If you are perceived as having a positive *"can do"* attitude, doors will open. If you are perceived as a *"negative Nelly,"* doors will also open, unfortunately they will likely have an EXIT sign over them. Perceptions may be based on fact or feelings. Either way, they are powerful.

History is rife with examples of perceptions, both imaginary and real. The grand and glorious Wizard of Oz was perceived by the Munchkins as an all-knowing, all-powerful being until Toto exposed the man behind the curtain. Another example is Adolf Hitler. German President Paul von Hindenburg appointed him Chancellor of Germany in 1933. The German people perceived him to be infallible, allowing his rise to untethered power. His reign lasted until 1945 when he blew his brains out sitting alone in his bunker. Today's media is expert at creating and shaping perceptions, especially of our political leaders. Perceptions are either based on feelings or fact.

It is not what you do but what people think you do that is important. The point is that each of us is viewed through the lens of someone else's perceptions. It is important for you to understand how your boss, peers, and subordinates perceive you. Ask for help if you can't figure it out on your own. A good way to do this is through a 360 Degree Evaluation. Those you work with (boss, peers and subordinates) are asked to evaluate you in a private, confidential manner. The results of this feedback will be eye opening and possibly painful to come face-to-face with. Remember, perceptions are based on the combination of feelings and reality.

You have the power to change perceptions. If perceptions are based on feelings, modify the relationship. If they are based on fact, change the reality. For example, you may feel you are the most open and sharing person in the office. However, your peers perceive you to be aloof and unapproachable. You need to work on acting more grounded and take the time to sit and sincerely talk and share a little with them. On the other hand, if you are perceived as smelling bad and looking disheveled, change the reality by showering daily and finding someone to improve your physical appearance and wardrobe.

You worked long and hard learning how to perform the tasks you were hired for. However, your college classes may not have taught you how to fit into the social structure of the workplace. If you want to keep the job and grow to higher levels of responsibility and financial rewards, you need to become a reliable, responsible member of the team.

Read on...

Chapter 2: Communicating Effectively

The ability to communicate effectively is the key to moving your career forward. It is how we share ideas and convince others to follow us. We will examine the three basic forms of communication: written, spoken and body language.

<u>How you say what you say counts!</u>

Know your audience. Whether presenting in written or oral form, the first step of communication is to understand the vernacular of your audience. Vernacular is the everyday language and slang used by a group of people and will differ from the official language in use. Even though everyone is speaking the same official language, various words, phrases and visuals may not translate to everyone in the same way.

Sports analogies are often used in the U.S. to accentuate our message. I recall quite vividly a meeting with my Indian colleagues. We were discussing a particular project that was nearing a decision. We needed to decide to either continue the project or scrap it. The speaker (from the U.S.) said, "It is late in the fourth quarter and we either need to go for the gold or punt the ball." Even though everyone in attendance spoke formal English, the folks from India thought the message was strange. First, since the meeting was held in the *first quarter* of the year they did not understand why the speaker was talking about the *fourth quarter*. Also, they did not understand how *gold* became involved with the project. To this day they are still confused about what a *punt* is since there is no such animal involved in the game of cricket.

The more global your audience is, the more diverse the language differences will be. This is especially so with the use of slang language. Be prepared to understand that some words have different meanings based on geography and the group that uses them. In the U.S. for example, a *"beamer"* is short for a BMW automobile. In the U.K. it is slang for a projector. The question, "Where can I park my pinto" will be met with snickering in Venezuela where "pinto" refers to the male organ. To assure your message is understood correctly, you need to test your audience on their knowledge of slang. Written and verbal communication causes the most confusion for an audience with diverse backgrounds. Try making important points without using slang. Including a variety of phrases helps. Don't be afraid to ask your audience to communicate their understanding of the topic back to you.

When using projection slides to help convey your message in front of an audience, be sure to follow a few basic tips.

- Make sure you use a font that can be read clearly from the back of the room. Experiment with different fonts and sizes. Test it in a similar venue to make sure it is readable.

- Avoid putting too many words on each slide. Use bullet points to capture key thoughts, not the excruciating detail.

- Certain color combinations really "pop" giving your presentation a professional look and feel. There are also color combinations that look awful. If you can't tell the difference, ask a co-worker to give you a critique.

The tone of the message. When speaking, the tone of your message can change how it is received. The phrase, "it is not what you said, but how you said it" refers to the mood (anger, animosity, etc.) and body language of the presenter.

Consider the phrase, "I thought I told you, do not sit on the sofa." The listener's perception of this phrase changes based on the tone and inflection imparted by the speaker:

- "I thought I told you, do not sit on the sofa." Said calmly, this would usually be considered to be a non-hostile message. It simply warns the listener to not sit on the sofa for it might be wet, soiled or in poor repair.

- "I THOUGHT I told you, do not sit on the sofa." The tone of this message emphasizes the word "thought" and may include physical gestures like pointing your index finger, raising your voice or making a fist. It could be heard by the listener as "You idiot, do you have the brains of a chicken? How many times do I have to tell you not to sit on the sofa?" The tone in this message is condescending and may be a bit threatening.

- "I thought I told you, DO NOT SIT on the sofa." The tone in this message emphasizes the "do not sit" directive. When said while standing over the listener, it is an obvious projection of anger and definitely threatening.

Body language – the universal form of communication! "Sit up straight, don't slouch, and look someone squarely in the eye. And for heaven's sake stop the yawning!" It turns out Mom was right. Body language expresses feelings and emotions to the person you are communicating with. The message body language sends is as important as what you are saying. Remember this in your next job interview. This topic was probably touched on in your introductory psychology class. However, given the impact it will have on your career, I suggest that everyone take the time to do a quick web search (or use the library if you are old enough to remember how to do that) to understand the messages your body language is sending. Here are a few common examples of what your body language is sending that you may not be aware of.

- *Eyes:* Looking to the right may mean fabrication or lying. Looking to the left typically signals recalling or searching for facts. Direct eye contact indicates attentiveness and interest in what the speaker is saying.

- *Arms:* Folded indicates defensiveness and reluctance. Gripping own upper arms shows insecurity. One arm across the body clasping other arm signals nervousness. This is more often observed with the ladies.

- *Hands:* Palm(s) down sends a signal of authority, strength and/or dominance. Interwoven clenched fingers indicate frustration, negativity and anxiousness. Hands in pockets express disinterest and boredom. A firm handshake will show confidence.

- *Legs:* A seated person typically aims knees towards the point of interest. The converse is also true. They will be pointing away from someone you do not find interesting. Legs crossed can indicate caution or disinterest.

- *The space invasion:* It is important to understand what "personal space" is and the correct physically distance to keep between you and other people. Personal hygiene is also important when discussing closeness to others. The technical term for the personal space aspect of body language is "proxemics." Edward T. Hall devised the word in his 1963 book, <u>Proxemics, A Study of Man's Spatial Relationship</u>. It is about the distance people find comfortable between themselves and others. Hall describes five zones that apply to Western societies.

  Close Intimate: 0-6 inches. It is for lovers and those engaged in physical touching relationships. Make sure you do something about your breath and general level of cleanliness so you don't send off alarms!

  Intimate: 6-18 inches. Reserved for intimate relationships, close friendships and contact sports. It may also apply to crowded places such as parties, bars, concerts and public transportation. Intrusion into this space may be uncomfortable and threatening. Within the intimate zone a person's senses of smell and touch become especially acute. Remember to brush your teeth and use deodorant.

Personal: 18 inches – 4 feet. Touching is possible in this zone, but intimacy is off-limits. Touching someone you don't know very well (other than a simple handshake) is likely to be uncomfortable. Before hugging everyone in the office, make sure you know how the person you are about to hug will react.

Social Consultative: 4-12 feet. Hand shaking is only possible within this zone and only if both people reach out to do it. Touching beyond a handshake is generally not acceptable unless both people reach to do it.

Public: 12+ feet. People establish this space when they seek to avoid an interaction with others nearby. When another intrudes this space it creates an uncomfortable expectation of interaction.

- *Miscellaneous:* Your overall posture says a lot about your level of interest in what's going on. When you lay back, put your hands behind your head or generally slouch, you are saying that you are not interested or *"buying into"* what the speaker is saying. Yawning is perhaps the single most blatantly negative body language message. It says, "I don't care about what you are saying, you are putting me to sleep here!" Yawning may be the result of insecurities and/or exhaustion. Regardless of why you are yawning, keep in mind the message is going to be the same – you do not care what the other person is saying.

Some of the elements of body language discussed above may vary due to differences in various ethnic groups. For example, when someone's head nods up and down it usually signals agreement with what you are saying. In India, the head nod indicates that the listener *understands* what you are saying but doesn't necessarily signal *agreement*. Hand gestures are not consistent across cultures either. Be careful!

Facial expressions are interesting and seem to be uniformly understood across the globe. Charles Darwin was an early pioneer in the study of facial expression. In 1870 he hypothesized that facial expressions were universally understood across all cultures but he was never able prove his theory. Nearly 100 years later Dr. David Matsumoto, from San Francisco State University and Dr. Paul Ekman of the Paul Ekman Group LLC, Oakland, Ca. were able to conduct studies that confirmed Darwin's theory. Their research suggests that people, regardless of cultural upbringing, universally understand expressions of happiness, anger, fear, sadness, disgust and surprise. Of all the various languages used around the world, understanding body language, and especially facial expression, is important for your success. Keep in mind that your body speaks volumes even when your lips are not moving.

Keeping cool!

Manage your temper! The most important piece of advice regarding communication is to never, ever, lose your temper! This is especially true when that anger is aimed at your boss, co-worker or employee. When you lose it, one of two things will have to happen; you will either lose your job or you will need to apologize to those you offended. Now, apologizing doesn't sound nearly as bad as being fired does it? However, the act of apologizing erodes your personal power.

Everyone in the workplace has some level of power. The power you have is a combination of *"position power"* and *"personal power."* Position power is job specific. Certain responsibilities and privileges were bestowed upon the job when it was created. These activities provide the latitude to do certain things that others can't do. For example, the boss has position power that allows him to review your personnel file, evaluate your performance and award your merit increase. Others are not allowed to do that. Position power is also associated with the rank of the individual; the higher the rank, the greater the power.

Along with position power is something known as personal power. Personal power is earned, not granted. It is based upon the respect you have gained from those around you, coupled with their desire to follow you. People with a high degree of personal power are amazingly influential and often become unofficial leaders. When you lose your temper, your personal power drops a few notches. Nothing is gained by losing your temper, so keep it under control!

Where is your anger targeted? When your temper tantrum becomes a direct personal assault on someone you work with, you need to ask those you offended to forgive you. Speaking from personal experience, this is not a pleasant task. Everyone has a bad day now and then, but losing your temper often, and *"bullying"* your co-workers, simply cannot and will not be tolerated.

Sometimes anger is directed at situations or specific events rather than individuals. Triggers may include: the value of the stock in your retirement fund suddenly drops; situations outside the company (i.e. a recession) require actions that may not be easy to adjust to; some sort of procedural mistake was made. Apologies for temper outbursts associated with these have a lesser impact on your personal power. However, it still puts co-workers on edge and can eventually impact your success.

You can't un-ring a bell. As noted, once you lose it you cannot simply take it back. The only way to un-ring this bell is to apologize. So if you are a chronic hothead you are probably wondering what advice I may have to help keep from losing it. Before you blow a gasket, try these on for size:

1. *Practice keeping your cool.* Fear is one of the key reasons we lose it. The fear of losing something (status, prestige, money, power, etc.) drives the need to protect our turf. Perhaps anger results from the adrenaline released during the *"flight or fight"* response. Remember, just a few thousand years ago our ancestors were living in caves, fighting off wooly mammoths and escaping the jaws of saber-toothed tigers. The survival of the human species benefited from adrenaline in those days and can also be useful today. However, in the modern-day workplace it is

important to counter the adrenaline rush resulting from political issues by keeping cool and not reacting with anger. Remember Mom's advice, "count to ten, and do it again." Good decisions are rarely made when angry.

2. *Practice keeping your cool.* My philosophy is that there is only one "best" solution to any problem. I used to get peeved when my co-workers didn't see things the same way I did. People tend to agree with what makes sense according to their frame of reference. The reason your solution is not the same as mine is that we may be looking at the problem through different experiences and personal history. The best way to get others to agree with your position is to take the time to educate them so they develop a similar frame of reference. Be patient, decisions are based on a lifetime of experiences. There will be times when you just can't create a common frame of reference with those that do not agree with you. In those cases, at least try to understand why your views are different. That doesn't mean either one of you is wrong. It simply means you are different. Vive la difference!!

3. *Practice keeping your cool.* Let's face it. Most of us have a life outside the office. Occasionally bad things happen in your personal life, creating an emotional state of mind that carries over into the office. Your kid is not doing well in school; there is not enough money to pay the plumber; your basement has just flooded and then one of your co-workers suggests something profoundly stupid! You snap. Those in the office see you losing it but don't see the stuff falling apart at home. When things do pile up in your personal life, it may be helpful to confide in your boss before doing something you will regret.

4. *Practice keeping your cool.* Instead of losing your temper, try responding with facts and figures. Office politics is a game and your objective is to win by outsmarting your opponents, not bludgeoning them to death. When you react in an angry manner the game is lost. Use words, facts

and figures to bolster your position rather than bullying your way into winning. This keeps emotions and personalities out of the equation.

5. *Practice keeping your cool.* You don't always need to be right. Sometimes the other person may have a better idea. Give them a chance to explain their position. Who knows, you might actually agree with it. The office is a political jungle. Agreeing with others builds alliances that may come in handy some day.

6. *Practice keeping your cool.* When you lose your temper you might win a minor battle, but eventually you will lose the war. You need to ask yourself if the anger is worth the price you have to pay. In most cases it is not worth losing the war (or your job).

What you say can (and usually will) be held against you!

When you speak badly about someone – it will get back to you! Nothing said in or about the workplace will ever be held in confidence. It just doesn't happen. If you enjoy an awkward situation, try explaining to your boss why you told your co-workers she was the worst boss ever. Or try explaining to one of your subordinates why you described him as not being the brightest bulb on the tree. Or try getting one of your peers to help with your project after you just described him as being "Dumber than a box of rocks." When talking about your co-workers, staff or boss, make sure you use positive language regardless of what the evidence says about that person. When in doubt heed your mother's advice, "If you can't say something nice, don't say anything at all!"

Electronic communication is not private! Every piece of email, texts and other forms of social media (Twitter, Facebook, Linkedin, etc.) you create can be circulated at the speed of light over the web. You can rest assured that employers, as well as envious co-workers, will search the web to learn as much about you as they can. Whatever dubious information you put out there can (and will) come back to haunt you.

Knock off the multi-tasking – Please! **People feel good when others show interest in what they are saying. It is flattering to the presenter if the listener is connected to the conversation. You may have experienced this. The problem is that many of today's new hires grew up during the burgeoning age of personal communication devices. Smart phones have become affordable and integrated into our daily routines. They make it possible to communicate with anyone, anywhere, anytime. Unfortunately, the technology grew faster than the proper etiquette for using it. For example:**

- Using your phone is extremely rude when meeting face-to-face with others. Texting, checking email, looking at the weather, checking scores, etc. all disconnect you from the conversation.

- Mute your phone and keep it in your pocket when in the office. Only use it for business or emergencies.

- Cell phone conversations in public places have no place in public places. Excuse yourself and move to a more private place if you must use the phone.

You may be thinking, "I'm able to manage two conversations at once." Take a moment and think about how this is being perceived by those around you. They are thinking, "That text (or tweet or whatever) is more important than I am."

Knowledge is power!

Respect the fact that people can confide in you. Every sizeable organization has a structure designed to facilitate internal efficiency. As you progress through your career path, you will be exposed to more and more confidential information. In order to become a trusted member of the team, you must respect this privilege. I'm going to repeat this: respect confidentiality. Your boss and the rest of the organization will have no use for you if you cannot be trusted. *(On rare occasions there are "whistle blowers" who break the bonds of confidentiality when they share privileged information in a public forum. Before you decide to blow the whistle make sure you have evaluated what will happen next, especially to you and your career. Ask yourself, "What good will come from my sharing this information?").*

Usually the confidential information you are privy to is associated with financial results, new product ideas, market campaigns, etc. This information will have a positive affect on business results especially if confidentiality is maintained. Remember, financial results must be shared in accord with the rules established by the Financial Accounting Standards Board (FASB) and/or the Security and Exchange Commission (SEC). Violation of these rules can result in termination and perhaps a prison term.

Respect the chain of command! You report to your boss, your boss reports to her boss, etc. This is the chain of command. As it relates to communication, it is important to respect the chain of command and not do an *"end around."* This is a sports analogy, specifically from American Football. An end around is a play designed for the person with the ball to run around the blockers instead of through the blockers. Although effective on the football field, it could result in your demise in the office. When you skirt around the chain of command going directly to the boss's boss, nobody will trust you again, especially your boss's boss. Avoid the temptation to do this even if the guy you work for is a certified moron. You must respect the chain of command and realize that every flat tire eventually gets changed; including the moron you work for.

Although precarious, you may be called in to discus your boss with your boss's boss. This could mean your boss is toast or it could mean the boss's boss is trying to support him. (The boss's boss may have put him in his current position). If this happens it is best to be honest, remain respectful and speak positively. Avoid throwing your boss under the bus.

Chapter 3: Understanding Organizational Structure

The Shape of the Organization

Wait a minute. I thought you said this book was about keeping my job and managing my career? Relax Max, this is not a book about Business Management. However, in order to grow and manage your career, you need to understand how the workplace is structured. More importantly, you need to know precisely where you fit into the process and exactly what the expected output of your job will be.

The essence of a *"for profit"* business is to produce a product or service and sell it in the marketplace with the intent to earn a profit from it. To achieve that goal, organizations are comprised of various combinations of the following functions aligned under the Chief Executive Officer (CEO).

Marketing and Selling:

The marketing group figures out what the marketplace will buy and at what price points. This is accomplished by evaluating the elements involved in promoting and selling a product including: market research, pricing, advertising, packaging, manufacturing and sales. The result is a volume forecast, budget, and rollout plan for a new product.

The sales team works with customers to demonstrate how the product can help them achieve their objectives. They need to understand how a product functions so they can assure the customer's requirements are met. They manage promotional budgets, develop proposals and bring in orders for the products the firm sells.

The V.P of Sales at one of my past employers had a great saying, "Nothing happens until you sell something." I thought this was just his way of pumping up the sales force. However, he was correct! Most organizations are built to *respond* to selling a product or service. It does no good to produce a product not in demand. For example, you may have a highly developed manufacturing process to make buggy whips. Unfortunately there is not a big demand for these and you probably won't sell too many. The sales force meets face-to-face with customers convincing them to buy what they need from our manufacturing process.

Operations – doing what the company does:

The primary role of Research and Development (R&D) is to develop new products and make improvements to existing ones. They create product and process specifications for the manufacture of items to assure quality and cost standards are met. They also design and manage consumer test panels to determine what (if any) preferences consumers may have as product alternatives are developed. R&D also collects and interprets data indicating how products are performing in the market. Part of the R&D role is to stay up to date with new developments in materials and processes.

The Materials Management function manages all processes, from purchasing raw material, to the shipment of finished goods to the customer. It assures that machines, staff and materials utilized efficiently. They monitor environmental, health and safety issues and interact with other corporate functions such as marketing and finance. This function is responsible for planning how much product to manufacture in order to meet anticipated market demand. The resulting plan is the Master Production Schedule (MPS). The MPS drives a number of sub-processes.

Staffing requirements, based on the MPS, are used to decide how many workers are needed. This results in hiring and/or layoff decisions.

Purchasing works with external vendors to assure an uninterrupted flow of materials to meet the MPS.

The Capacity Requirements Planning (CRP) process develops long-range strategies to assure the firm has the manufacturing capacity it needs to meet demand, well into the future.

The Quality Assurance (QA) team monitors the input and output of the production processes to assure that finished product meets or exceeds the standards expected by the customer. Their metrics and recommendations are used to improve the various steps in the production process.

Distribution and Logistics manage the physical flow of stuff across the supply chain: raw materials going into plants and finished goods coming out of them. They also manage the delivery of finished goods from Distribution Centers to customer warehouses.

Support Functions:

When you examine the basic functions of any company you will always find operations and sales. All of the other groups support these two primary functions.

The Financial Management and Accounting function assures that current operating results and future decisions achieve the profit goals of the company.

Financial Management has two primary functions. The first is to evaluate capital projects and investment proposals. They make sure these projects meet the firm's hurdle rates for Internal Rate of Return (IRR) and Return on Investment (ROI) objectives. The second is to analyze the performance of the firm and forecast future product cost to project earnings. This involves the balance of working capital dedicated to production assets, inventory, cash flow, credit levels, sales projections, production cost, etc.

Accounting is responsible for capturing all records needed to pass an audit. This includes receipts and expenditures needed to prepare, analyze and interpret financial statements. A recap of accounting documents are widely used among managers, investors, tax authorities, executives, and many others to see how the company is performing.

The Information Technology (IT) function is responsible for the design, implementation and maintenance of the firm's technology and computer systems. IT is comprised of three primary areas: *Governance* provides operating parameters for both individuals and functional units using IT applications, networks, architecture, and security. *Infrastructure* manages operating networks, telephony and equipment used to make the IT system work. *Applications* create computer system tools that enable employees to efficiently perform their tasks. This includes development, support and database design activities.

Human Resources (HR) is responsible for recruiting new hires and helping managers develop existing staff. HR helps with the creation of consistent job descriptions and salary levels across the broader organization. They are also involved in labor contracts, industrial relations, training, management development and disciplinary matters.

Each function identified above has a supporting structure of direct staff as well. The structure defines the process flow for decision-making. Knowing how decisions are made is the first step toward understanding how to get things done. This knowledge is vital for your career growth. So chill and try to relate to this chapter.

External Services:

Chartered Accountants typically visit clients as part of an audit team. They review operational and financial records to validate the company's accounts, offering advice on various exposures.

Management consultants are used to identify and investigate problems ranging from corporate policy, organizational structure and procedures used in the day-to-day operation of the company. They will recommend changes to improve results and provide implementation assistance as needed.

Recruiters (headhunters) assess job seeker skills, and for a fee, match them with employer vacancies.

Advertising Agencies work with their clients on marketing communications. They present proposals to boost sales via advertising campaigns while maintaining the firm's public image. The agency also manages the client's advertising budgets and keeps them up-to-date on competitor activities.

Market Research is a function that large firms may choose to do on their own. However, this function requires a deep level of practical expertise. Using a third party could result in a better, faster perspective at a lower cost. The primary roles for this function include: planning market research projects; analyzing specific problems (i.e. why are sales dropping); and creating proposals for the client. The research group also prepares and administers questionnaires and market surveys to better understand consumer trends.

A Public Relations (PR) firm suggests how certain aspects of media exposure may reflect on the public image of the firm. For example, they help prepare corporate brochures, press releases and press briefings. They also work with clients when image improvement is warranted due to a misstep by one of the key officers of the company.

<u>Span of control – Narrow, Wide, or Optimal.</u>

Power of the pyramid! Organizations tend to be shaped like pyramids. The person at the top (the Chief Executive Officer a.k.a. the CEO) has a team of individuals reporting directly to her. Each of them in turn has a team of individuals reporting to them and so on down to the bottom layer of the pyramid. Why all the layers? The span of control (number of people managed by one person) has limits. The answer to the question, "What is the optimal number of staff a person can manage?" is this, "It all depends."

Some organizations are flatter than others and have a wider span of control. Other organizations are narrower with fewer direct reports per manager on average. There are many factors influencing the organization shape (narrow vs. wide) and therefore the number of direct reports a supervisor can effectively manage; i.e. his or her span of control. The span can influence communication protocols, job satisfaction and even the organization's culture.

Narrow Span of Control – Advantages:

- A narrow span of control means each supervisor has fewer direct reports to manage.

- With less staff, the supervisor is able to spend more time developing each individual employee.

- The career path will be more clearly defined with more opportunity for upward mobility and advancement.

Narrow Span of Control – Disadvantages:

- Expense is higher due to more management layers.

- Supervisory involvement and potential micromanagement may result in less empowerment and delegation.

- Communication could be more difficult given the number of layers between the top and bottom of the organization.

Wider Span of Control – Advantages:

- Fewer reporting levels will result in an organization that is flatter, more flexible and nimble.

- This is ideal for supervisors with the primary role of answering questions and resolving employee issues.

- It encourages empowerment by delegating responsibility and decision-making power to employees.

Wider Span of Control – Disadvantages:

- Leads to overloaded supervisors when employees are new and inexperienced. They require a great deal more task direction, training and supervision.

- Inadequate nurturing of employees may lead to decreased morale and/or job satisfaction.

- It may be a challenge to find supervisors with the breadth of knowledge required to manage multiple functions.

Optimal Span of Control:

Establishing a *"one size fits all"* standard number of direct reports without understanding the nature of the business is irresponsible. It would be similar to expecting that an automobile will always travel at 30 mph without regard to driving conditions, posted speed limits and the skill of the driver. Even within a firm, some departments are better suited to a wider span of control than others. Modern organizational "experts" (steeped in academia) suggest the right number is about 15 to 20 subordinates per manager. Although there are certainly some managers with that many direct reports, this is not a realistic number for all managers. Those with practical experience suggest that 5-6 direct reports is the ideal number.

A recent research study by Gary Neilson and Julie Wulf, on the number of direct reports for C-level positions (CEO, CIO, COO, CFO, etc.) was published in the April 2012 Harvard Business Review. Their research shows that the average number of direct reports for these positions has doubled from five, in the mid 1980's, to about 10 in the mid 2000's. They hypothesize that the ability to manage a larger number of direct reports has been enabled by improved technologies. Over that time frame, we have seen the adoption of many new tools including personal computers, word processors, email, smartphones and teleconferencing.

Another study conducted by the Employers Resource Council (ERC) suggests the ideal span of control is anything but a *"one size fits all"* answer. The right number is unique for each function within the organization and will depend on various factors including:

- *Organization size:* The size of an organization greatly influences span of control. Larger ones tend to have wider spans of control than smaller ones.

- *The organization's culture:* The culture of an organization can influence the span of control. A more relaxed, flexible culture is consistent with a wider span of control, while a hierarchical culture is consistent with a narrow span of control. It is important to consider the current and desired culture when determining the span of control.

- *Nature of job:* Low complexity jobs require less supervision than jobs that are inherently complicated. Loosely defined jobs however, require more frequent managerial input than those that are highly structured. Jobs needing less supervision usually have a wider span of control. Jobs needing more supervision have narrow span of control.

- *Manager skills and competencies:* Supervisors with more experience can generally manage wider spans of control than those with less. Consideration should be given to individuals responsible for managing others and, at the same time, are required to perform a portion of the actual work duties.

- *Employee skills and abilities:* Less experienced employees require more training, direction, and delegation (closer supervision, narrow span of control) than experienced employees do (less supervision, wider span of control).

- *Type of interaction between supervisors and employees:* High interaction between supervision and their staff requires a narrower span of control. Less interaction, or supervisors that primarily answer questions and help solve occasional problems, is characteristic of a wider span of control. As you determine the span of control for an organization, you must understand the level of interaction that will exist between supervisors and staff.

- *Extended Staff:* Finally, you must consider the size of a manager's extended staff. Extended staff is defined as the employees that report to each of the manager's direct staff. A good manager maintains an active dialog with the extended staff to create a cohesive team. For example, if a manager has 10 direct reports, and each of those direct reports has 10 direct staff, there are 100 people in the extended team. The extended staff does not require the same level of interaction as direct staff, but spending just 30 minutes with each of them once a month consumes 50 hours or approximately 1.5 days per week! Maintaining a dialog with the extended staff is critical for new managers and/or newly formed functions.

Designed for internal efficiencies

I've been on hold for 40 minutes! As a consumer, have you ever been stymied when confronting large organizations such as insurance companies, governmental bodies, colleges, etc.? These organizations are typically designed for internal (rather than customer facing) efficiencies. In order to manage the internal chaos, companies design, implement and enforce structured protocols. Managers in these organizations are evaluated for how well they process and pass tasks from one function to another. Rarely are they evaluated for how well they deliver services to external customers. Unfortunately, the external consumer is left alone to face the maze of contacts before they finally reach the one individual that can actually solve their issue. That is, of course, assuming the consumer has the time, patience and tenacity to stay on the line!

Eventually the customer will decide to give up their quest for services (insurance companies thrive on this strategy to minimize claims they would otherwise pay) or switch to a new service provider if they can. Sometimes customers do not have the option of moving to a new service provider. When the customer is captive, why would a company spend money to retain them? Insurance companies (especially when the employer pays for the policy), colleges and governmental bodies have little to gain from being customer focused. As a result, they typically are not.

The opposite is true for those companies in industries where consumers can easily switch providers. Cable providers, retail stores, hotels, etc. are in fierce competition for the customer. It is more cost effective to retain the customers they have than it is to replace them. As a result, they have developed sophisticated customer retention processes in order to retain their customers.

Why are bosses needed?

Are we all children or what? Why do I need a boss? Your boss and your boss's boss (hopefully you will become one some day) are the link between you and the top of the house. As organizations grow, the number of people in them grows too, as do the layers between the top and bottom. Those at the bottom are the ones engaged in daily face-to-face contact with customers. To optimize effectiveness, the organization's business strategy must be clearly and consistently linked all the way to the customer-facing employees.

Solid linkage, from top to bottom, utilizes the power of the pyramid. For example, if each manager has ten direct reports an organization with 10,000 people would have four layers. The person at the top may make million dollar decisions each day. There are approximately 9,000 people at the customer-facing level. If each one makes a $1,000 decision each day it amounts to $9 million dollars! If the CEO has communicated the business strategy down to every layer in the pyramid, these decisions will optimize results. If management layers under the CEO are not aligned, these $1,000 decisions can have a negative impact on business results.

Your boss should assure alignment between you and the other parts of the organization you need to interface with. The task you perform requires inputs from upstream processes. Your job is to convert these inputs into outputs. Each function relies on the preceding function for inputs. When the inputs to your process are flawed, so then will be the outputs you create.

When your outputs are not up to par, they will create issues for the next function. A failure in any part of the system will have a domino affect on all downstream processes. Your boss is the official liaison between you and those functions you interact with. We will get into more detail on this in the next chapter.

Finally, your boss assigns tasks and jobs that need to be done in support of the over-arching business strategy. The ideal boss will do three things:

1. Assign the task you need to accomplish.

2. Provide the resources needed to complete the task.

3. Get out of the way.

Chapter 4: Managing Your Job

What is a job anyway?

What am I doing? A job is a combination of actions and activities that result in a desired output. People often confuse the word *"job"* with *"position title."* They are quite different. When you browse websites for employment, you see a list of open position titles such as: accountant, nurse, supervisor, sales director, etc. The actual work activities associated with each of these positions is detailed and varied. Position titles are fine to use on business cards, or drawing organization charts. Can you imagine trying to fit all of your job duties on a business card? In order to understand the specifics of a job, we have to identify each of the tasks associated with it. These tasks are generally *"-ing"* words.

Does the work I do end with "ing?" One needs to understand the *"action"* words that describe the actual work elements of the job. For example, *"accountant"* is a title with many variants, each with their own duties. A *"cost accountant"* is proficient at collect<u>ing</u> data, defin<u>ing</u> product cost (labor, materials, overhead, etc.) and identify<u>ing</u> ways to reduce that cost. (Note all the *"ing"* words!) An accountant that works in the *"payables"* department will be performing a different set of tasks. They stay busy establish<u>ing</u> a 3-way match by validat<u>ing</u> the purchase order, verify<u>ing</u> the price and quantity on the invoice and assur<u>ing</u> the receipt of goods or services has occurred. Although they are both called *"accountants"* their daily tasks are radically different.

Job titles are daunting for someone new to the organization. New hires should ask to see a *"job description"* showing all of the activities they are responsible for. A job description helps clarify precisely what you were hired to do. It is important to realize that job descriptions are not cast in stone and may change as the needs of the firm change. Warning: crafty managers may attempt to add more activities to a job and fluff up the job's title. This tactic adds prestige and more work but may not include additional salary!

Every job is part of an overarching process!

Know how your job fits into the overarching process. There are firms in which a single employee does every task, from procurement to sales. These are sole proprietorships with no employees. We will focus on firms with employees that work on teams with other employees to deliver a final output.

(Although our discussion focus is on the latter, it is interesting to note that sole proprietorships, specifically those without any employees, represent a large portion of the U.S. labor force. According to the U.S. Census Bureau (2010) and the Bureau of Labor Statistics, small businesses comprise 50% of all private sector jobs in the U.S. 75% of them have no employees.)

Your job is a process that converts *"inputs"* into *"outputs."* Some are more obvious than others. Here are a few examples:

- A sculptor converts raw clay (*input*) by shaping it with his hands (*process*) into a vase (*output*).

- A radiologist converts imaging scans (*input*) by analyzing abnormalities (*process*) into medical opinions (*output*).

- A mayor converts the desires of the populace (*input*) by prioritizing them (*process*) into municipal work (*output*).

- An actor converts the script (*input*) by acting (*process*) into a believable role (*output*).

Let's examine the simple process of grinding coffee beans to make a great pot of java. The process of grind*ing* coffee is vital when brewing a great cup of coffee. In order to produce a high quality brew, the grind size of the output is important (too large means less flavor, too fine results in a clogged filter). Also, the freshness of the ground coffee is critical as flavor deteriorates rapidly once the ground beans are exposed to air. Don't grind next week's coffee today. Only grind enough for the next pot.

The quality of the output from the grinding process is subject to its inputs. The person grinding the coffee can basically control grind size and freshness. However, the age of the beans, degree of roasting, moisture content, and other "*upstream*" attributes are not within the control of the grinder. A process can be analyzed to understand how its output may be influenced by its inputs. Total Quality Management (TQM) evolved as a combination of data and tools used to improve quality. The SIPOC analysis is one of those tools. SIPOC examines the interrelationship between process elements: Suppliers –> Inputs –> Process –> Outputs – > Customer.

Let's focus on the inputs first. The supplier (or suppliers) to your process may be an external vendor, another department within your firm or both. The supplier's output is your input. In order to deliver a quality output you must work with each supplier to assure they understand the input requirements your process needs in order to create a quality output.

You need to know your process well enough to define input "*standards*" and be able to express them so they are clearly understood and measurable. For example: *To meet the Hawaii Department of Agriculture standard for green coffee, the moisture level must be between 9 and 12 percent.*

The supplier must be confident that his or her process is capable of delivering these standards in a statistically reliable manner. As a customer, don't accept standards from a process that is incapable of delivering them.

Old school quality management programs inspected the finished product to assure it met standards. Measuring the output is fine but the damage has already been done. A more effective practice is to measure the inputs as they enter the process. This data can then be used to alert you if something changes in your supplier's process. It will also facilitate a fact-based discussion (rather than an argument) with the supplier and hopefully will help them resolve issues and improve their process output (your input!).

Let's look at the <u>output</u> of your process next. The customer of your process may be external, another department within your firm or both. Since your output is someone else's input, you must make sure you are delivering at acceptable levels of quality, quantity, timeliness, etc. You need to work with the customer to establish standards for your output. As noted above, you need to make sure your process is capable of delivering these standards. If it is not, can it be modified so it can deliver the requested standards in a sustainable manner? How much will modifications cost?

Example: You are managing an industrial oven that tempers metal by heating it. Your customer requires the metal reaches 700 degrees (plus or minus 5%) and holds at that temperature for 35 minutes. First, you must check to see if the oven can even attain a temperature of 700 degrees. If it can, does your research indicate it is able to maintain that temp within a 5% tolerance for 35 minutes? If your process is not capable of consistently meeting the desired standard, you need to share that information with your customer. At that point a decision needs to be made to change the process, change the standard or use a different supplier. Process capability is a key concept to understand. Never agree to a standard for a process that is not capable of meeting it.

Let's examine <u>your</u> process: If your job ends in "ing" then you are doing something. In order to better understand your process, I suggest using another TQM tool known as the *"Fishbone Analysis."* It is called a Fishbone Analysis because it looks like the bones in a fish. It is a useful tool that allows us to conceptualize a process to understand its process flow. It helps us understand the key internal elements that affect its ability to convert inputs into outputs. In the following fishbone analysis, we will assume that the inputs meet specification. Therefore any issues with output result from one of the internal process constraints: Procedures, Labor, Machines and Technology. Each process may have a unique set of constraints from the next. However, there will be constraints to identify and manage.

Fishbone Analysis

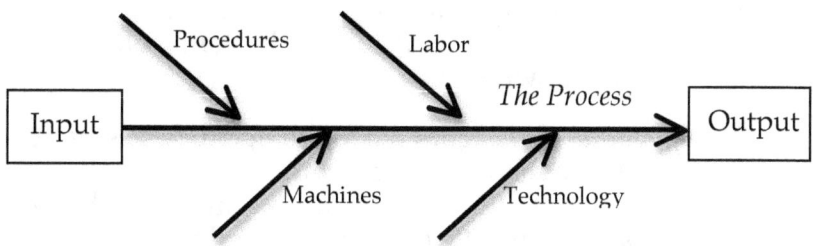

Applying the Fishbone analysis to any process will help to better understand the constraints at play:

- *Procedures:* Standard Operating Procedures (SOP's) are written to assure a process is repeatable with the ability to function in a consistent manner. The use of SOP's will result in optimized equipment performance as well. Questions to ask: Are SOP's meeting the specs of the manufacturer? Have operators been properly trained on these procedures? Is the process monitored to assure SOP's are followed? Are they updated as needed?

- *Labor:* Labor is important to every process. Naturally, a complex process requires a higher level of job skills than one that is less complicated. We can "dumb down" the skill level needed by decomposing a complex process into a series of easy-to-follow mini-steps. However, we need to carefully balance the intelligence required by the job vs.

that of the worker. Consider the following quote by Herman Wouk from his classic novel, *The Caine Mutiny*:

> *"The Navy is a master plan designed by geniuses for execution by idiots. If you are not an idiot, but find yourself in the Navy, you can only operate well by pretending to be one. All the shortcuts and economies and common-sense changes that your native intelligence suggests to you are mistakes. Learn to quash them. Constantly ask yourself, "How would I do this if I were a fool?" Throttle down your mind to a crawl. Then you will never go wrong."*

A high labor turnover rate is a chronic problem impacting both output and quality. It is usually the result of one or more of the following conditions:

Over qualified: This occurs when the operator's skills are at a higher level than what is required by the job. These people may opt to find a more challenging job rather than, as Wouk says, "Throttle down their mind to a crawl."

Underpaid relative to other firms: Supply and demand for a certain skill causes pay levels to change. Firms will attract new hires by offering higher than average pay. Soon, a migration between firms begins.

Environment: Bad working conditions are a predictor of turnover. A good environment entices employees to stay even when the work is sheer drudgery. Relationships with the boss and co-workers are also important.

- *Machines:* Machines can perform a task with a high degree of precision and speed, complimenting the human worker. Questions to ask: Is the machine properly maintained and adjusted? Is it performing as designed? Are there adjustments and/or upgrades available that would enable it to operate better? How much capital investment and time is required to reach the desired output? Has the machine come to the end of its useful life? Does it need to be replaced?

- *Technology:* Keeping pace with ever-changing technology requires an investment in time and money. Too often, due to budget issues, this investment is not made, or at best, deferred to future years. New technology keeps evolving while the old continues to deteriorate thus, widening the gap between them. Those clinging to the old technology are disadvantaged in their market as it becomes more difficult to remain competitive. At some point the vendor will stop supporting the old technology creating a major risk to operations. When this occurs, a major investment is needed to upgrade to current state.

Pareto Analysis. The Fishbone Analysis will provide a number of issues to work on, but it is difficult to know which to work on first. Pareto Analysis helps prioritize your efforts. This rule states, "eighty percent of your trouble will come from 20 per cent of your problems." This means that each problem rarely has the same impact as the next. Therefore, it is best rank them and concentrate on the most important ones first.

The essence of the rule is to look for *"the vital few issues"* with the most impact, separating them from *"the trivial many."* Identify which particular problems are the most important by collecting the appropriate data and displaying it in a histogram. The measured characteristics will be displayed in descending order. Such a histogram is a Pareto Diagram.

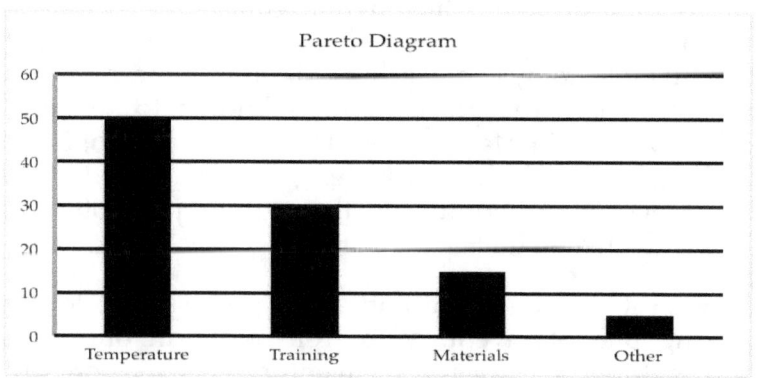

The "Temperature" issues on the left hand side of the histogram have a greater impact than the other issues. They should be worked on first. Pareto's rule, also known as the 80/20 rule, was named after Vilfredo Pareto. In the late 18th century, Pareto studied the distribution of wealth in Europe and found that 80% was held by 20% of the population.

Although TQM tools such as SIPOC, Fishbone, and Pareto Analysis are used heavily in manufacturing processes, they can also provide value in non-manufacturing processes.

Improving process throughput.

Manage the bottlenecks! Throughput is the amount of product a process produces over a given time. The bottleneck of any process sets the pace for the entire process. If you improve the throughput of a bottleneck process, throughput of the entire process will improve. There will always be bottlenecks and as soon as one is resolved another takes its place. In his book, The Goal, Eliyahu Goldratt does an excellent job explaining productivity improvement by focusing on bottlenecks. I strongly recommend reading it. Although published in 1984, in 2011 The Goal ranked #10 on Time Magazine's list of the "25 Most Influential Business Management Books."

Focus investment only on bottleneck processes. Investing in a non-bottleneck process will not improve throughput!

Consider a process in which two machines, "A" and "B" each perform an activity on the product. If Machine "A" processes 100 units per hour, and Machine "B" only processes 80 units per hour, the actual throughput is limited to 80 units per hour. Investing in Machine "A" to make it faster only results in a larger pile of inventory waiting for Machine "B" to do its task. Machine "B" limits the throughput pace of the total process to only 80 units per hour.

The easiest way to spot a bottleneck process is to look for a growing pile of inventory in front of it. In our example, process B follows process A. Inventory grows before process

B because A produces faster than B. Since the bottleneck dictates total throughput of any system, management should balance processes by improving bottlenecks. This keeps inter-process inventory to a minimum thereby reducing inventory investment (cost) without slowing output. This is known as a *"fixed"* sequential process in which B must always follow A.

Golf offers a different example in which process steps (holes played) can be arranged *"independently"* from each other. Why do we find an *"inventory"* of golfers waiting to tee off on some golf holes? Golfers patiently wait to tee off until the preceding group takes their second shot. A nine-hole golf course typically has 2 Par 3's, 2 Par 5's and 5 Par 4's. On a busy day, the inventory of golfers seems to grow fastest at Par 3 holes. Is there an optimal sequence to arrange these nine holes to maximize the number of golfers in play, thereby improving throughput and increasing revenue? According to my brother Joe, (who plays golf just about every day and has recorded 9 holes-in-one!) there is.

Major resorts start with Par 5's or an easier Par 4 with generous fairways and easier greens. This maximizes the number of players that can be started per hour.

The length of each hole is adjusted by using multiple tee boxes. The longer the hole, the more time it takes to finish. When golfers play from the proper tee box for their ability, play goes faster.

Par 3's are shorter. The next group to tee off must wait until the green clears thus building an inventory of golfers at the tee box.

Tee shots go faster than players chipping or playing out of a sand trap. The slowest play on any hole (the bottleneck) is putting.

The best way to increase throughput (revenue) is to enlarge the hole from the regulation $4^{1/16}$" diameter. Play will go much faster.

Effective managers are skilled at identifying bottlenecks and know that when one is resolved, another takes its place. In our machine example, if we improve the pace of Machine B to

120 units per hour, the bottleneck shifts to Machine A as it can only produce 100 units per hour. Consumer demand may also be a bottleneck. You will know that demand is a bottleneck when finished goods inventory starts growing in the warehouse. Avoid making costly production investments if the demand doesn't warrant it. *Remember, investing time and money in a non-bottleneck process will never improve throughput!*

Are you a bottleneck? One of the more common concerns I hear is this: *"My plate is full and work keeps coming in faster than I can get it done. My boss is not willing to add extra staff to help get it done."* First of all, the inventory of jobs piling up in front of your process indicates a bottleneck. Being overloaded is a morale buster and should not be taken lightly. Before we declare the boss to be an idiot (and she might well be one) for not providing more resources, we need to look a little deeper. There may be something else causing this bottleneck.

Parkinson's Law: You may be experiencing Parkinson's Law. In 1955, Cyril Parkinson articulated, *"work expands so as to fill the time available for its completion."* If your work group feels overworked yet continues to find ways to get the work done on time, Parkinson's Law may be the culprit.

Assume a specific job requires four hours of pure work effort to complete it correctly. However, you are given eight hours to complete it in. With the extra time, additional steps that are not really needed are added to fill out the eight hours: conferring with others; re-checking quality; and excessive testing fill the available time.

Soon, the job consumes eight hours. If it had been performed correctly the first time, none of these incremental steps are productive or needed. The operator, believing it really takes eight hours for one job, becomes overwhelmed when a second job is dropped on the plate. These two jobs should only take eight hours to do correctly. The extra activities, now deemed critical to the process, make it feel like sixteen hours are needed.

If the group continues to find ways to get these jobs done, it indicates they are taking shortcuts somewhere, hopefully on extraneous activities. My advice is to take the time and analyze all the process steps (Fishbone?). Differentiate *"core activities"* from those that can be eliminated. It is possible that new core activities have been added resulting in more time required to finish the job. These will show up in the fishbone analysis and can be addressed to order to better balance workflow and resources.

Under-skilled labor: Firms may hire employees that simply do not have the skills required to finish the job correctly in the allotted time. This may be done to lower costs or because people with the required skills are not available. Outsourcing portions of the work to a third party results in a steep learning curve before the resources are fully capable. The bottom line is this: it will take longer to finish the job and any re-work produced. The ability to get the job done in four hours is no longer possible.

OK, the boss just might be an idiot! Sometimes the boss just doesn't understand the processes well enough to effectively manage them. That knowledge gap may result in situations where the staff becomes over-loaded. You need to support the boss even in difficult times. Poor decision-making and resulting bottlenecks will eventually be addressed. It is best to stay out of that melee.

You can manage anything; you just can't manage everything! The ability to balance priorities is similar to managing bottlenecks in that their relative importance is in a constant state of flux. Since time is a fixed constant (there are only so many hours in a day) it should be allocated to those priorities most in need of attention that day.

Keep your priorities in front of you. I mean that literally. Write them down on a sheet of paper and hang it on your bathroom mirror so they are in front of you every day! List your priorities and know which needs your attention now. One of your personal priorities may be a healthy relationship with your family and friends. Every so often, spending time with them may be the most important thing!

Understand your point of difference

Always know what distinguishes you from everyone else that does what you do! Each person is a priceless individual that should be respected by everyone in the workplace. That is different than saying everyone should be paid the same, regardless of the work they do.

In a free economy, pay for certain jobs is a function of the supply and demand for the skills required to produce the output of that job. Interestingly, pay is independent from the intrinsic value of the output itself. As an example, most would agree that receiving quality healthcare has a greater intrinsic value than watching professional football on Sunday afternoon. However, the *minimum* salary for a professional football player in the NFL with five years in the league was $715,000 in 2013, dwarfing the average pay of family practice doctors in the U.S. The top players are paid millions.

It is all driven by supply and demand. When demand for an item, skills in this case, increases faster than the supply, its price (salary) will increase. The reverse holds true as well. When the demand drops, so will price. Logic would suggest that one should learn to capitalize on this fact. In order to be paid more, you need to either:

- *Develop* skills to perform work with high demand: graphic designers, pharmacists, actuaries, recording engineers, etc.

- *Differentiate* yourself from others offering similar skills by combining complimentary activities such as video *and* sound editing.

- *Dedicate* yourself to high levels of perfection. Perform the job better, faster and at a lower cost than everyone else doing the same work.

In the final analysis, pay has little to do with what's fare. It is a function of the demand for skills and the degree of difficulty finding and replacing those skills in the market.

Example 1: *Unique skills*

There was a town with a nuclear reactor located nearby. One day, the reactor started to overheat. It was on the verge of a core meltdown. Technicians at the reactor tried to correct the condition but did not know how to resolve it. The condition was getting worse. A core meltdown would destroy the town, resulting in millions of dollars of damage. Finally, within a few hours of the meltdown, an expert was called in. He evaluated the situation and after 15 minutes approached the control panel, pushed one button and resolved the situation. He then gave the mayor a $40,000 bill for his services. Naturally, the mayor argued that pushing one button was not worth $40,000. The expert responded, "My unique skills resulted in knowing the correct button to push. Continuing to push the wrong buttons would have cost you millions!"

Example 2: *Why are salaries for elementary school teachers so much less than what we pay college professors?*

Few jobs are more important than educating our children. The grade school teacher works long hours preparing lesson plans, meeting with parents, and spending all day long in the classroom. They are role models with our children clinging to every word they speak. In the child's eye, their teacher is their world! Teachers are paid a low-to-average salary but, for the most part, have decent benefits.

On the other hand, the average professor earns twice what a grade school teacher earns yet spends only 3-6 hours per week in the classroom. The balance of their time is spent on research, counseling students, and publishing. One could easily argue this salary model is upside down.

However, it reinforces the fact that pay is independent from output. One's value is a function of the availability of their skills vs. the intrinsic value of the output. Perhaps the 3 P's help to explain the pay difference between elementary school teachers and college professors.

- *Preparation:* The elementary teacher requires a four-year degree in education. A professor requires a Ph.D., which takes many years of study and research.

- *Prestige:* College professors, who are recognized experts in their field, bring prestige to the institution. This is important for attracting donations from alumni et al.

- *Profitability:* Top professors at research institutions can bring in millions in grant money. The school's financial structure relies heavily on these grants, rewarding those professors who are able to attract them.

As we examine the price paid for certain services, the 3 P's explain why a plumber is paid $80/hr. while the urologist earns $400/hour. After all, they both work on pipes. The 3 P's can also explain large pay packages for surgeons, entertainers, sports figures and CEO's.

- The surgeon's skill is difficult to replicate as it takes years of study and practice to develop.

- The CEO of a major company is responsible for creating, implementing and maintaining successful business plans that result in profit for the shareholders as well as jobs for many people.

- The pay for entertainers, politicians, sports figures and performing artists is based on their inherent skill, level of dedication and the preparation required to become the best in their field.

The pay someone receives is a function of the difficulty to replace his or her skills. It has little to do with what the firm is able or willing to pay. Keep this in mind when you evaluate the pay *you* should receive.

Manage your time wisely

Good time management skills: Individuals possessing good time-management skills are better equipped to provide reliable estimates for the time it will take to complete a task. This helps them gain notoriety for the on-time delivery of projects. The ability to manage your time wisely may help distinguish you among others and increase your value.

What is the most important thing I should be doing right now? If you ask this question frequently and answer it honestly, you are managing your time well. Time management is all about understanding your priorities and knowing where to focus your attention right now. Your "number one" priority may always be number one. However, the amount of time you need to spend on it may change each day.

Are you bored doing the same job day after day?

Am I ready for a change? If you answered this question with a "yes," congratulations, you are normal. It is natural for us to get bored with our jobs. A job-performance lifecycle defines your relationship to your job. The three basic phases of the lifecycle are: induction, perfection, and optimization.

Induction: This phase is also called a *"learning curve."* During this phase we learn all we can about the job. The more complex the job is, the longer the learning curve. People learn at different rates but eventually most of us get through the induction phase and are able to perform the basic tasks of the job. Naturally there will be "bad hires" that simply do not have the skills required for the job. They will eventually be reassigned to a different job or perhaps, a different employer.

Perfection: Once trained, the individual's performance level will grow to a point where cost, quality and output improve. As discussed earlier, the output of a process should have defined standards for quality and quantity associated with it. By the end of the perfection phase, the employee should be able to meet or exceed these standards.

Optimization: During optimization, the employee creates a theoretical operating model based on his or her accumulated knowledge, process rules and environmental constraints. A theoretical operating model is a set of rules that describe how a process functions. Modeling within these rules will allow us to generate improved methods and predict how a process may react to environmental changes. This helps us define acceptable tolerances to inputs and outputs as well.

For me, it takes about three years to work my way through the job lifecycle. The first year is spent learning the finer points of the job; the second is perfecting job performance; and the third year is when process improvements move into high gear. This is about the time I start looking for, and in many cases designing and creating my next job assignment.

Chapter 5: Managing Paradigms

Success breeds success – doesn't it? Not always. Sometimes success breeds failure! Reality shows that a valley lies beyond every peak. It has to or else it wouldn't have been a peak in the first place. Organizations must be prepared to challenge their existing paradigms, adapt to new ones and keep moving forward. If not, it is extremely likely that past successes may lead to failure.

What is a paradigm?

A paradigm is a model or set of rules that help us understand the environment we live in. When the current paradigm changes, people will initially feel uncomfortable. However, change is inevitable and when it occurs, the resilience and adaptability of the human spirit is amazing. In time, people not only accept but begin to thrive in their new paradigm.

As an instructor, my lecture on *"Change Management"* started in the very first class meeting by assigning a *"permanent"* seat to each student. I told them it would be their seat for the semester but not that it was part of an experiment. I explained it was the best way for me to associate their names and faces. Three weeks later I changed the seating chart. Grumbling ensued immediately. After three more weeks passed, I exposed the experiment during my *"Change Management"* lecture. The discussion on why they reacted the way they did revealed the following: Soon after the initial seat assignments were made, they adjusted to it and found comfort in knowing where their seat would be, "So we didn't have to come to lecture early!" They also adapted to the view of the podium from their seat and who they were seated next to. When the seating chart changed, they had to re-adapt and re-learn what they had grown comfortable with. Although none of them were happy with the change, they were able to adjust to the shift in their paradigm.

Paradigms exist on many levels and may not be immediately obvious. A few years ago I attended a lecture by Professor John Donovan (MIT). Professor Donovan explained that an important technological innovation might shift a business to a new paradigm. That shift often results in rewards of wealth and power for those responsible for the innovation. They are frequently promoted into decision-making positions as well. These people will do whatever it takes to preserve their status and actually work to prevent changes to their original idea. Once comfortable, they fear that changes to their paradigm may result in a loss of prestige and power. New ideas were met with skepticism and were sucked into what Donovan labeled the "black hole of comfort," never to see the light of day. At this point the firm is sheltering itself from all outside change. New ideas and innovation stop. The end is near.

Paradigms can provide insight about how we believe our environment behaves. People feel safe when they follow and adhere to the rules that define their world. Children are born without inherent paradigms or fears. Challenging everything, they often learn the rules and realities of our world the hard way. They quickly learn not to touch a hot stove and also learn the rules of gravity. These rules create boundaries around the *world we know.* The boundaries blind us to anything that may exist outside of our comfort zone.

Paradigms can be bad if they limit our thinking and blind us to what might be possible. You may have heard about the experiment in which fruit flies are placed in a jar. Without a lid they will eventually find their way out through the top of the jar. However, if you place a lid on the jar, they soon come to realize flying out of the jar is not possible. Even when the lid is removed, they will not try to fly out because they have *"learned"* they can't. This experiment exposes a paradigm affecting the fruit fly's behavior. That paradigm suggests that escape through the top of the jar is not an option. When paradigms limit our thinking, we stop exploring alternatives that may exist in the *world we don't know*.

Paradigms can blind our search for innovative solutions. Our collective base of knowledge is defined by what we know and what we don't know. For example, *we know* that nuclear fusion occurs when two atoms collide at a very high speed. They fuse together to form a new type of atomic nucleus. Our sun's energy is the result of such collisions between hydrogen nuclei. The reaction creates helium atoms and releases heat energy. What *we don't know* is how to contain the reaction in order to harnesses the energy produced from it. Someday the problem of containing a fusion reaction will be solved. The scientific community is working hard to find an innovative solution for this problem. Just like other innovations, it will come from the world *we didn't know we didn't know*.

Paradigm Paralysis

When we become comfortable in our paradigms, we lose sight of the possibilities that exist *"outside the box."* Over the years I have observed that most people in the organizations I have worked in accept *"what is"* as the only way it *"can be."* Few of them would purposely suggest changes that might challenge the status quo. Those entrenched in the old world are the ones that create *"black holes of comfort."* They will actively ignore, ostracize and expel anyone who tries to change it, thereby protecting the old way of doing things.

Speaking from my own experience, the role of *"change agent"* can be a difficult one. It is amazing how fast obstacles are created and heels become dug in when ideas for change are presented. The change agent can either be an employee or a third party consultant; it doesn't matter. What does matter is this: to be successful, the change agent needs an endorsement from top management. For example, to implement change in the IT department, the Chief Information Officer (CIO) must endorse and support the change agent.

Every organization has certain operating rules defining the world in which it exists. However, once paradigm paralysis sets in, the world will often pass it by. A competitor's innovation may challenge foundational paradigms. These once described the old market in which the organization had thrived. When the paradigm changes, everyone goes back to zero. Prior success means nothing.

In 1962, Thomas Kuhn wrote <u>The Structure of Scientific Revolution.</u> In it he fathered, defined and popularized the concept of a *"paradigm shift."* Kuhn argues that scientific advancement is not evolutionary, but rather is a "series of peaceful interludes punctuated by intellectually violent revolutions." In those revolutions, "one conceptual world view is replaced by another" when the paradigm shifts.

Kuhn defines a paradigm shift as a "change from one way of thinking to another. It is a revolution, a transformation, and a sort of metamorphosis. It doesn't happen on its own, but rather, agents of change drive it. For example, agriculture changed early primitive society. Native American Indians existed for centuries roaming the earth, hunting and gathering seasonal foods and water. However, by 2000 B.C., Middle America was a landscape of very small villages, each surrounded by patchy fields of corn and other vegetables."

Johann Gutenberg was an agent of change when he invented movable type in the 1440's. With the invention of the printing press, books became smaller, easier to mass-produce, less expensive to purchase, and more readily available. The printing press significantly changed our culture and directly contributed to the scientific revolution.

Agents of change are driving new paradigm shifts today. The signs are all around us. For example, the introduction of the personal computer and the Internet Browser has impacted both personal and business environments. It is the catalyst for a paradigm shift. We are shifting from a mechanistic, manufacturing, industrial society to an organic, service based, information-centered society. Advances in technology will continue to impact us globally. Change is inevitable.

Success can only breed success in organizations that resist the urge to reinforce their "black holes of comfort." In order to remain open to new ideas and prevent paradigm paralysis, organizations need to create an environment in which people are not afraid to fail. Innovative ideas should be rewarded, not stifled. Every existing paradigm needs to be challenged and occasionally changed. In their book, <u>If It Ain't Broke – Break It!</u> Robert J. Kriegel and Louis Palter endorse a philosophy that constantly challenges the existing way of doing things.

Per Thomas Kuhn, "mankind has been evolving for millions of years and will continue to do so. Human Beings resist change; however, the process has been set in motion long ago and we will continue to co-create our own experience. What we perceive, whether normal or metanormal, conscious or unconscious, are subject to the limitations and distortions produced by our inherited and socially conditional nature. However, this does not restrict us for we can change. We are moving at an accelerated rate of speed and our state of consciousness is transforming and transcending. Many are awakening as our conscious awareness expands."

<u>Recognizing and managing a paradigm shift</u>

When the paradigm changes, everyone goes back to zero! The theoretical operating model described in the prior chapter is great for making marginal *evolutionary* modifications to an existing process. However, by its very nature, evolutionary change only works if the operating paradigm remains stable. Knowing the rules and how various actions should interact gives us comfort. It is human nature to want the paradigms explaining our world to remain unchanged.

Eventually however, anomalies will begin to appear that do not fit the accepted paradigm. Initially these are ignored by the majority and are labeled *"quirks"* of nature. Historically, the definition of *"good management"* was a philosophy of top down leadership. Those at the top, insulated by layers of staff, make decisions that determine the direction the business will take. However, top-line decision makers are furthest from where these *"quirks"* occur, making it easier for them to ignore their existence. Additionally, their livelihood is based on maintaining the status quo rather than rocking the boat. The individuals close to these *"quirks"* see them as a sign the world is changing. They are often labeled *"kooks"* or worse. Organizations want to expel them just like an organism tries to expel a foreign bacterium it sees as a threat to its existence.

The anomalies continue. Growing more and more prevalent they confound the accepted world of knowledge as well as those that once thrived in it. The tipping point is eventually reached and a paradigm shift occurs. Those clinging to the old technology have nothing except fond memories of that which was. A paradigm shift is a *revolutionary* change and firms that miss it go back to zero paying the price in lost revenue, profits and market prominence.

Everyone knows the sun revolves around our Earth! The Greek philosopher, Aristotle (384–322 B.C.) proposed a geocentric model of the universe in which the sun and planets revolve around Earth. This continued to be the accepted astronomical theory for the next 1,500 years.

However, anomalies began to appear as man created more accurate tools to observe what was happening. Tables used to predict astronomical events (such as an eclipse) were deemed to no longer be sufficiently accurate. Also, the calendar, instituted by Julius Caesar in 44 B.C. was no longer accurate. At the time of the Council of Nicea (325 A.D.) the equinox fell on the 21st of the month. Twelve hundred years later it slipped to the 11th of the month. Europeans looked to the astronomers to solve these problems.

Heretic! Nut Job! The astronomer, Copernicus (1473 – 1543) dared to posit a different view of the universe. In his book, <u>De Revolutionibus Orbium Coelestium</u> ("On the Revolutions of the Celestial Orbs"), he described a heliocentric model of our solar system in which the Earth and planets revolve around the Sun. The anomalies observed in the geocentric model formed the foundation for this new thinking. The scientific community and the Catholic Church as well, rejected the new heliocentric theory of Copernicus. Nevertheless, the old paradigm had begun shifting. It took the next 150 years for the old science to be replaced by the new.

The many scientific discoveries and inventions of Galileo (1564–1642) included the telescope. Galileo used it to provide evidence that supported the Copernican theory of the Earth revolving around the sun. This did not sit well with the Catholic Church and in 1633 Galileo was called to Rome to face the Inquisition. Today, Galileo Galilei's middle finger is encased in glass in the Florence History of Science Museum, Florence, Italy. Many suggest it is his final tribute to the condemnation he suffered at the hands of the Inquisition. Thanks to Galileo, the Copernican model is the accepted paradigm today. That is, until some crackpot changes it!

The business world is full of examples where major paradigm shifts were missed, often leading to a company's demise. Clayton M. Christensen's book, "The Innovator's Dilemma" documents a number of market-leading companies that have missed game-changing transformations in industry after industry. Examples include computers (mainframes to PCs), telephony (landline to mobile), photography (film to digital), and video recordings (Beta to VHS to DVD to Blue Ray). Firms missed the shift because they made huge capital investments based on their existing (old) frame of reference. They never saw the future coming. Instead, they missed innovations that would deliver blockbuster products, open new markets and attract new customers. By sticking to their old paradigms, they completely missed out on opportunities in the new world.

The trick of course is to figure out which anomaly will result in the next paradigm shift vs. the ones that are nothing more than, well, anomalies. Firms need to encourage innovative ideas and *"outside the box"* thinking. They need to accept the occasional failure and reward employees for identifying the next paradigm shift *before* it happens! Once in a while, firms need an infusion of new blood in order to be able to "see the forest for the trees" making it easier for them to recognize anomalies to existing paradigms. Hindsight is always 20/20, whereas the future always seems cloudy.

Emeritus Professor, Rodney Von Behren (OMU), had a penchant for decorating the walls of his office with thought provoking signage. Although I have lost track of the individuals these quotes are attributed to, I thought I would share with you a few of my favorites:

> "If all you ever do is what you have always done, you will never move forward."

> "The definition of insanity is doing the same thing over and over expecting different results."

> "It is not the strongest of the species that survives, nor the most intelligent that survives. It is the one that is most adaptable to change that survives."

> "Life is tough, but it's tougher if you're stupid."

Chapter 6: Selling and Negotiating

Selling wreaths during the Holidays

Many years ago I was contemplating the work I would be doing when I grew up. Becoming a salesman was at the bottom of the list. When I was a kid I had to sell wreaths during the Holidays in order to raise money for my Boy Scout troop. Maybe I was soured from knocking on every door throughout the neighborhood and getting a vast number of "No's" from people. Maybe it was asking people to give me ten dollars for a wreath. (To this day, asking for something, anything, including directions is still distasteful.) I didn't see the benefit I was providing. After all, if someone really wanted a holiday wreath on their door, they would have gone out and bought one for themselves. I couldn't see why they needed my services.

The idea of asking a stranger to hand over money for something they didn't want in the first place was repugnant. No way, a career in sales was not for me! I did not realize it at the time, but selling would be one of the most valuable skills I could have developed. Effective selling helped my career in many ways. From the very first day you are hired, you are selling yourself and your ideas.

My first real job after college was a production supervisor. The hiring criteria for line supervisors had more to do with size than scholastic achievements. At 6'2" and 250 lbs. I was a natural! It was years later when I finally realized that using my imposing size was not an effective way to get things done. I had to learn how to sell.

Success comes from solving someone else's problem. My idea of selling was based on the *buyer doing something for me!* It took some time for me to realize that successful selling has nothing to do with "high pressure" tactics associated with selling used cars or insurance. It is about presenting a compelling solution that solves a problem the buyer is experiencing; a solution that "scratches the buyers itch." You have to make it perfectly clear that the solution you are selling will solve a problem the buyer is facing. I'll say it again, the right perspective for successful selling is to *solve a problem for the buyer*.

The fact is, we each have to learn how to sell ourselves. As a job seeker, one needs to learn how to sell their skills to a future employer. That employer needs to be convinced that more than anyone else, you can fill the requirements of a particular job. To do this, we must first convince (or *sell*) ourselves that we have the unique skills and experiences to solve the hiring manager's problem.

Once on the job, our successes become the basis for future promotions and raises. The essence of every job is to manage a process, produce a desired output and solve problems that hinder that process. The track record of output and solving problems becomes the basis for one's resume. Keep track of these. Success also builds confidence in one's abilities and confidence (rather than arrogance) is a desired trait that managers look for in job candidates.

<u>There is only one solution to any problem… yours!</u>

Whoa! Talk about arrogance. During the course of a career, you will face problems that interfere with processes you manage. The solutions we synthesize to solve these problems may be self-contained, meaning that another process is not impacted by them. However, it is frequently the case that our solution will impact someone else's process. If you do not believe your solution is optimal, how can you ever convince anyone else that it is? Let's take a moment and think about how we form perspectives about certain issues.

- The perspectives we form are based on unique events and experiences we are exposed to during our lifetimes.

- Some of these experiences are more impactful than others. Whether good or bad, they will be with us for a long time.

- Some are top of mind while others are subliminal. Yet, each experience will shape how we view the world.

- The cumulative affect will heavily skew how we feel about issues as well as the best way to resolve them.

Given the vast number of individual events each of us will be subjected to over our lifetime, it is highly improbable that our set of experiences will be identical to anyone else's. Our perceptual constancy, based upon these experiences, explains why two people will either agree or disagree on an issue. We believe that our solution is optimal because our experience tells us so. People agree with our point of view when their experiences are aligned and similar to ours. They will tend to disagree when their experiences differ greatly.

One way to convince someone to do what *you* want to do is to bully and use brute strength to force the acceptance of your idea. Brute strength (position power in the workplace) can only be effective on subordinates or those who are weaker. Your team will do whatever you tell them to do, for fear of being fired. They may fear you, but not really respect you. They will never fully buy into the concept you are forcing upon them and will not support it emotionally. Even worse, your team may throw common sense out the window and do exactly what you tell them to do. Following the exact letter of any directive, without the temperance of common sense, can yield devastating results. Pushing your subordinates around is bad enough but pushing your boss or peers around may result in *your* early departure.

A better way to convince others to do what you want is to educate and *sell them* on the idea. Filling in the gaps to more closely align their history of experiences with yours helps develop a unified view. In this way, you can sell them on why you believe your idea is best. Bear in mind that sometimes, your perspective may be the one to get changed by the experiences of others! A few examples:

1. *Where to produce a new product?* I was asked to identify the best facility in which to manufacture a new product we were preparing to launch. I was to present my findings to the leadership team. My suggestion was to utilize our plant in the Los Angeles area for this purpose. I knew ahead of time that my boss and the other decision makers would not like this solution. Their perspective was based on the high cost of modifications the plant would need in order to produce the product. Since my position did not grant me the power to force my suggestion, I set about filling in the gaps in their histories hoping to change their perspective.

I studied the proximity of the plant to both raw materials and where finished product would be delivered. I found that the location of the Los Angeles plant provided significant transportation cost advantages for both inbound raw materials and outbound shipments to customers. Also, labor rates at this facility were lower than other sites. Since the product was labor intensive the lower rates generated additional savings that favored this plant. The facts about the cost advantages convinced my boss that the optimal solution was to use the Los Angeles facility. Once my boss was aligned, she was able to help sell the idea to the other decision makers. A decision was made to invest in the modifications at the Los Angeles facility. It grew to become the largest manufacturing facility for this product!

2. *The business trip.* I was scheduled for a meeting in Texas on Monday and Tuesday and had to be in our Chicago office for a 9:00 am meeting on Wednesday. My options were to take a red-eye flight to O'Hare on Tuesday evening, arriving just after midnight, or get up early for a 6:30 am flight Wednesday morning, arriving at O'Hare by 8:00 am.

My initial thought was to take the red-eye flight. However, before booking the flight I ran the idea past one of my female colleagues. Her suggestion was to get up early and take the 6:30 am flight noting that O'Hare at midnight could be a rather threatening place. Never having been in O'Hare at midnight, my history of experiences was incomplete. With better knowledge, I decided to take the morning flight.

3. Purchasing Software. There are two financial components to consider when purchasing computer software. One is the *capital* expenditure to cover the price of the software itself. The second is the ongoing *expense* paid to the vendor each year for maintenance of the software. This is typically 18% of the purchase price.

> Note: Capital expenditures can be amortized over five to seven years, whereas the annual maintenance is an expense that must be fully budgeted and paid for each year.

I was negotiating the purchase of a major software package with one of our vendors. We had reached an impasse on the initial price. Neither side was willing to moderate their position. The software salesman was paid commission based on some percentage of the purchase price. Further reductions in the price meant the salesman would have less commission. The other thing I knew was that the vendor was approaching the end of a very difficult year and needed to book as much revenue as possible to help their results. The revenue from our purchase could be booked in the year the contract was signed, but maintenance fees are booked when paid in the future. It turns out a higher purchase price was good for the salesman and the vendor.

Our finance team was far more concerned with finding the money to fund ongoing expense. Capital was more readily available. A price of $5 Million amortized over 5 years resulted in an annual cost of $1.9 Million: $1 Million for amortization plus $900,000 for maintenance at 18% of the purchase price. I conceded the $5 Million purchase price in exchange for a 50% reduction in the annual maintenance fee. The finance team and my boss jumped on board. By conceding the purchase price of $5 Million and dropping the maintenance fee to 9%, our annual cost dropped to $1.45 Million: $1 Million for the amortized cost of the software but only $450,000 for the maintenance cost. It was a three-way win: our team was ecstatic with the reduced expense, the software salesman got his full commission, and the vendor was able to book revenue.

<u>Support ideas with facts and data…avoid saying "I think."</u>

Nobody really cares what you think! When you use the words *"I think"* the discussion degrades into an emotionally charged personality battle. People will take issue with *"what you think"* and proceed to tell you what *"they think."* The lower you are in the pecking order, the worse this will be for you. Remember, everyone has a different history of experiences. Those you are trying to sell an idea to will more than likely *not* be aligned with your history. If they were aligned you wouldn't need to sell the idea to them in the first place. Assume that few, if any, in the room will think the way you do. Your mission, as the above examples demonstrate, is to align their history of experiences with yours. When you say, *"I think…"* those you are trying to sell will discount your opinion as simply that, an opinion.

Data talks, bulls--t walks! When you start your discussion with the words, *"the data shows"* instead of, *"I think"* the data become the topic of discussion, not your feelings. Data and facts are un-emotional and can be supported or challenged without creating animosity. The data exist and should be made available to whoever wants to observe and challenge them. The data itself (rather than you) becomes scrutinized if it supports your position. If the opposition accepts your data, that's fine, you win. If your data becomes challenged, those opposing it must refute it by presenting an alternative set of data. They can't just say, "I don't believe your data."

Can't I just use made-up facts? Only if you are a politician! It seems as though politicians are able to use faulty data and outright lies when they speak. I am sure you have heard the joke, "How do I know when a politician is not lying?" Answer, "When her lips are not moving!" Sad but true! If you are looking to have the credibility of a politician, go ahead and use contrived data. However, if you want to be credible, make sure the data you use to support your position is validated. If you don't take the time to validate your data, someone else will! Be sure to use multiple sources when you confirm your data. Using a single source, especially a contrarian one, can result in a flawed perspective. At the same time, just because one's perspective goes against the grain doesn't mean it is wrong. It may be the one person that sees the Emperor riding naked through town.

Sales and financial information are data generated inside your firm. This data may be easier to validate since those that created it may be available to discuss it. Also, internal data forms the basis for the firms financial and tax reporting. These reports must be accurate. Internal data may not always be easy to access and could require an IT expert to find, sort and extract it for you. You need to figure out what it means; how it is trending and how it relates to other data.

Beware of Web Searches! It is easy to do a quick web search on just about any topic. Always be suspect of what you find especially if it supports your position perfectly. The problem with web searches is that you have no way of knowing the credentials or competence of the person on the other end of the data. This makes it difficult to validate. Any two-bit scammer can create or clone a website that looks authentic. Crosschecking over multiple sites helps ensure it is consistent. Not necessarily accurate, but consistent.

Where do I find the data I need? The answer to this question is likely to be different for each person who asks it. As noted above, if searching for internal data on things such as sales, product cost, salaries, benefits, etc. I would start in your IT department. Typically data elements such as these will be found in data tables created for computer applications used across your company. Some data, such as salaries for example, will likely require authority to access. A good IT person can assist you by consolidating the data and presenting it in a database you can search. I always made sure I had a person with IT skills to act as the "data guru" for my group. Having access to data gives one the power and perspectives to make substantive changes to the organization.

Example: One of our product lines was subject to extreme demand volatility. A major volume peak occurred at the end of the 2nd quarter each year. The natural demand for the product was slightly higher in summer months than it was in colder parts of the year. Adding to this natural increase in demand, Sales and Marketing juiced up the pricing incentives paid to the retailers, resulting in huge shipment spikes. The retailers were quick to take advantage of the price incentives and "load" inventory in their warehouses. To fill the demand, our plants would work overtime and pre-build a large inventory to service those orders. This went on for years with each year being more severe than the one before. I still remember the Sales guys telling me that without price incentives they would not be able to hit their volume targets. Of course "I felt" the cost of generating the discounted revenue (inventory, overtime, storage costs, etc.) was not profitable. The Sales Department was king, my *feelings* lost.

However, using data, I was able to actually show what was going on. The cost and revenue data showed how deep price incentives paid to retailers left us a very slim margin. The reduced margin and costly overtime required to produce the product generated a net loss compared to normal times. The net loss was hidden because the cost of goods used was an average annual cost instead of an actual cost. Shipment patterns for each retailer showed they were holding the product in inventory much longer than normal. They had to hold inventory longer because the shipments were not selling through at store level. Retailers that would normally order each week would double or triple their orders and stop ordering for a few weeks until the glut of inventory was consumed. Finally, because the price reductions were not being reflected on the store shelf, consumer consumption was minimally affected by retailer price incentives. To sum it all up: consumers were not buying more because the price incentives were not reflected on the shelf. Retailers were pocketing the incentives and holding inventory. It didn't take long for our company president to change the selling practices. The drug of choice for many retail manufacturers is price and promotion. Once they are hooked, it is difficult to stop.

<u>Negotiating</u>

According to the Merriam-Webster Dictionary, "negotiation" is defined as "a formal discussion between people who are trying to reach an agreement." In many ways, the prep work for negotiating requires similar techniques as those used for selling. After all, it is all about convincing the other party that your perspective is right. Like selling, negotiation requires that both parties come together and agree on a set of criteria with which to move forward. A successful negotiator, just like a successful salesperson, is able to help people form a new perspective. The thing to keep in mind is when you are negotiating, both sides may need to moderate their objectives and give up something of value. This is often the case with selling too.

Negotiating is a useful skill to develop. It is not an exact science as the results may be somewhat unpredictable. One needs to approach a negotiation session in the same way an actor prepares for a stage performance. Sadly, similar to what happens when the actor is ill prepared, negotiations go awry when one fails to do their homework. You should expect that those across the table have done their homework and will come prepared to achieve their objectives.

Understand the goals of each stakeholder. The first step is to understand the landscape and identify the stakeholders. Each will want to gain something of value from the discussion and may or may not be willing to give up something near to get it. When the cost of the anticipated gain is too high, they will break away from the discussion. Figure out, in advance, what the breakpoint is for every stakeholder including you.

Leave your ego at the door. A good negotiator will take his or her ego out of the equation and think about the situation from the other's perspective. They will research industry trends, market concerns and key issues facing each stakeholder. In this way they can hone in on what might add value; not only for themselves but others at the table. It is not unusual for one or more of the stakeholders to be blinded, to a degree, by their paradigms. You may help them have an *"ah ha moment"* by revealing points of value they were not aware of. The successful negotiator does research in order to identify and suggest multiple points of value not on the *"radar"* of those across the table.

Use data and focus on results. As discussed earlier, using facts and data to sell your ideas avoids hostility caused by clashing personalities. Keep the focus of the negotiation solely on results, while working to create the best long-term *"win-win"* deal for all stakeholders. Taking the emphasis off of the people at the table and focusing on results will keep the discussion flowing. It will also improve the chances that an agreement will be reached that everyone can accept.

Good negotiators never loose their cool. Business negotiations often hinge on assigning a value to you or your product. It is not always easy to separate yourself from the issues under discussion. Most people you will negotiate with are smart enough to realize that you have something to gain from the discussion. They will translate a gain for you into a loss for them. When you become emotional and loose your cool, they will think you have a great deal more to gain than is obvious. This may cause them to dig in. Worse, they may respond by losing their cool as well. When discussion turns into rampant anarchy, it is time to turn off the lights, shut the front door and go home. Game over for now!

During negotiations, wisdom is a virtue! Successful negotiations require a mutual partnership to end up with a agreement that fits all stakeholders. Take the time to build a relationship by showing respect and understanding the needs of everyone at the table. Discussions involving mutual interests ensure that everyone will feel good about the end game. If you act in a respectful manner, it is very likely that those at the table will respond in similar fashion. Avoid ego-boosting tactics such as assuming a position of power, ridiculing others and acting narcissistic. These tactics demonstrate poor negotiating skills and will poison the relationship. Avoid these at all costs and stay focused on the end results.

Make your concerns known and define your boundaries. There are multiple constraints forming boundaries for an agreement under discussion. Expressing your concerns will help define what your negotiating boundaries are.

> Example: You are negotiating with your boss for a raise and share a concern about the needs of the family. This conveys the reason you want the raise (hungry kids) but doesn't force the boss into a yes or no answer. It helps the boss understand your situation. Alternatively, approaching the conversation demanding a 10% raise will force a yes or no answer and may effectively end the negotiation.

I want this, and I want that! Going on the offensive with the "I" statements creates a confrontational atmosphere. Those you are negotiating with will also post their demands and before you know it, the whole discussion begins to look like the U.S. Congress! Focusing on mutual results by saying things like "we need to reach a solution" helps keep the egos at bay.

Body language speaks volumes. Show that you are engaged in the conversation by leaning into it with both elbows on the table. Sitting back in the chair and slouching away from the conversation sends an "I'm not interested" message to everyone at the table. This is because leaning back instead of forward puts more physical distance between you and the others. All aspects of your personal communication (eyes, words and body language) must scream, "I'm engaged and want to find a mutually acceptable solution!"

"We beat them because they are inferior!" During your career there may be opportunities to negotiate with the same people multiple times. If you want things to go smoothly in future discussions, do not destroy or badmouth the opposition. When you win, be sure to praise your opponents and leave them some dignity. Take a lesson from successful coaches who are careful to never infuriate (and thereby motivate) their opponents by saying things like, "We beat an inferior team today." Or, "They lost because they don't know how to play." Creating animosity does no good and will always come back to haunt you. It gives your opponents one more reason to rise to the occasion to beat you next time. Also, if you happen to come out on the short end of the stick, learn to lose with dignity. Do not trash-talk those that beat you. Take a lesson from our elected officials and DO NOT do as they do.

Know when to hold 'em, and know when to fold 'em.

One of the fundamental errors parents are often guilty of is giving their kids an ultimatum (threat) they cannot or will not follow through with. "You better be good or you will not get presents for your birthday." Now what parent in their right mind will follow through with that threat? The problem is this: kids learn fast and realize when you are bluffing and have no intention of following through on your threat. The same is true when negotiating, especially those you negotiate with frequently.

Over the course a negotiation, ultimatums have the potential to become destructive because they require a corresponding action by one or both parties. An ultimatum such as, "Unless we reach a compromise on pay by November 10th, we will cease operations and shut the plant down" has implications for both sides. It leaves virtually no room to negotiate. If a compromise is not reached by the deadline, the plant is shut down and people lose their jobs. If labor gives in, they have to eat crow and explain to their side why they "lost." If management caves and doesn't close the plant, they eat crow. Unless you have a good recipe for crow, I would avoid taking a stand that you cannot (or will not) follow through with.

Perhaps we can take a lesson from our elected leaders in Washington. When you do find it necessary to back off of an ultimatum, make sure there is an outside factor causing your change in heart. Look for someone, or something, other than your own failure to blame. You may decide that you really don't want to move the plant and can moderate your salary position. Say something like, "Recently published research indicates new salary data and we are able to modify our position." This assigns the reason for changing your position on something beyond your control, new data.

The next one that talks loses!

When negotiating, a very powerful tactic is to state your position, shut up, and wait for the other person to speak. The discussion starts out with the two sides on opposite ends of the spectrum. If the negotiation is moving in the right direction, the two sides draw closer to an agreement. They draw closer by each giving incremental concessions. Taking a position that moves the sides farther apart is illogical. Once you agree to something, credibility is lost if you withdraw it. It is also illogical to give an unneeded concession. Why offer a second concession right after you just gave one?

Allow the folks on the other side of the table the time they need to evaluate your point and formulate a response. While they are doing this, it is critical that you stand mute. If you speak next, you need to give something up. Think about it this way; you just stated your position and before your opponent has had a chance to react to it, you open your mouth and change it. Since it is irrational for you to take something off the table, the only option you have is to give up more, which is illogical too. Here is an example:

> You are negotiating for the purchase of a new car. The salesperson says the price is $25,000. It is your turn to either

accept the offer or counter. You respond by saying you are only willing to pay $21,000. If you speak before the salesperson does, you can't say, "Wait, I'll only pay $20,000." That is an irrational response because you already committed to $21,000. The only rational response is for you to offer to pay more. Why would you do that? Once you state a position, wait for the other person to respond, regardless of how long it takes. If you follow this advice and refrain from speaking, the salesperson will need to take one of three options: accept your offer of $21,000; tell you to go elsewhere; or counter your offer by saying, "I can come down to $24,000." Now it is your turn to accept, walk or counter. The next one who speaks loses something.

You will be amazed at how effective this technique really is. Try it the next time you are negotiating something, anything, everything!

Chapter 7: Managing Others

<u>Managing people</u>

I find it interesting that many people do not understand the difference between *"management"* and *"leadership."* These terms are often used interchangeably, yet they are very different. Management focuses on the effective utilization of resources. It is *"how"* things should be accomplished. The manager sets goals and priorities, assigns work and meshes personalities along the way. He also has a fiduciary responsibility to the firm and monitors results. Leadership on the other hand is about creating a vision, setting future direction and motivating your people to get there. This chapter is focused on managing others. A future chapter addresses leadership.

Where do I learn how to manage people? Great question! At some point in your career you will have the opportunity to manage the work, whims and wishes of others. This is a big responsibility. Your actions will have an effect on the success and/or failures of your staff. It takes time to train someone to become an effective manager. Aspiring managers typically start with small teams and progress to larger ones over time. It would be insane to thrust a large group on someone with limited experience. Managing others is learned by doing.

<u>What is the role of your team?</u>

Why are we meeting? One of my childhood memories is that of forming clubs with my friends. Each summer as our long-awaited break from school began, we got the itch to start a new club. We elected officers and scheduled meetings. The first meeting was spent trying to figure out what our club would do. Even though we were young, we knew we needed a reason for being. It didn't take long to conclude that we had no reason to meet and by the end of that first meeting, we voted to dissolve the club. The following summer, with renewed energy and resolve, we tried again only to dissolve our club after the first meeting. We never found a valid reason for being. This memory stuck with me. To this day, I cannot get motivated until I know what my role and the role of my team is.

So, the first step in managing people is making sure they all understand their purpose. A clear purpose will guide them and help them understand where they fit into the process. They need to learn their role and how to navigate through the maze of company structure. Role definition is important, especially for recently formed teams. I suggest holding frequent meetings with the extended staff to get the message out and explain their purpose. I found it beneficial to invite my direct staff to participate in these meetings. In fact, they took the lead in presenting our strategies; training junior staff; and encouraging the team to ask questions.

The second thing an experienced manager will do is look for gaps and overlaps in decision-making. These are often found at the boundaries between teams. They exist when roles and responsibilities are not clearly understood. Gaps exist when an issue has nobody assigned to resolve it. Conversely, overlaps result when multiple teams are solving the same issue, creating costly inefficiencies. Here are a few examples:

Resolving issues: When more than one team believes that each is responsible for resolving an issue, stakeholders become confused about who is in charge and what advice to follow. One voice is best.

Informing clients: Multiple teams may each believe they are responsible for keeping their clients informed about active issues, solutions and next steps. Multiple messages create confusion and misdirection for the stakeholders.

Not my job: A gap occurs when a team believes someone else is responsible for a specific action or outcome when, in fact, no one is. I've seen this in baseball when a long fly ball falls between two outfielders. Each thinking the other guy would make the catch. Go Cubs!

An effective way to *"manage the margins"* is to bring together the teams working in a common space and develop a *"Roles & Responsibilities"* matrix. The result is a *"Lead, Participate or Inform"* (LPI) chart. The LPI chart becomes a great tool to inform all stakeholders who is supposed to be doing what, to whom, and when. LPI charts are created through discussion with all team leaders. The chart identifies which team will *"Lead"* the resolution of each issue. Their decision is final and all teams agree to support it. Other teams will *"Participate"* by providing input to formulate the best decision. Finally, those teams not directly impacted by the decision simply need to be *"Informed"* of the outcome. The LPI matrix is a constant work in progress. It should be refined when new questions and issues develop at the boundary between teams.

Set goals, secure resources, and get out of the way!

Is there a magic formula for managing? No, there is no magic formula but I have observed three things successful managers do: Set goals. Provide resources. Get out of the way.

Goal setting is important for a number of reasons. It gives your team a direction to follow. The team's goals will become the basis for evaluating their performance. In order to avoid conflicts and confusion down the road, goals should be shared with other parts of the firm so they know what your group is doing.

Goals give teams a firm direction to follow; a vision of what it is they need to achieve. Since goals often become the basis for performance evaluation, it is critical to discuss these goals with your team. Make sure they understand, accept and adopt them. I found it helpful to create S.M.A.R.T. goals: Specific; Measurable; Attainable; Realistic; and Timely.

Specific: Vague goals such as, "Improve revenue" or "Grow market share" are open to a wide range of interpretation. Avoid using goals that are vague and ambiguous by being as specific as you can be. Here are these same goals stated with more specificity: "By the end of the 4th quarter you need to improve revenue by 5% over prior year" or "By the end of each quarter, market share needs to increase by 2% over the same quarter from the prior year." With specific goals in front of them, teams will be able to create the action plans needed to achieve them. Since these goals contain *"by when"* statements, a delivery timetable can be created to help guide their work.

Measurable: Give your team specific goals so their results can be measured in an objective manner. The old adage, "In order to improve a process, measure it" is both true and very appropriate in goal setting. Good metrics are typically comprised of two dimensions: The first being the absolute performance achieved versus the objective. The second dimension is time. Example: "Increasing revenue by 3%" is a one-dimensional measure lacking a *"by when"* component of time. If a 3% increase occurs at the end of the 4th quarter, the team would miss the goal. However, if a 3% increase occurs by the end of the 2nd quarter, they appear to be on track to meet or beat their objective.

Attainable: This can be confusing. My suggestion is to focus on the *"degree of attainability"* possible. Approach this by focusing on the goal itself and ignore the experience and capability of the team for a moment. Improving revenue by 25% would be impossible for even the best of teams to achieve. Therefore, it is an example of an unattainable goal. Experienced managers know the degree of attainability for processes they manage. Clearly 25% is unattainable but what about 5% or 10%? Teams believe their leader is infallible and would never assign a goal that cannot be met. If they can't achieve a goal, they will feel that they failed, not you. Set your teams up for success by giving them attainable goals.

Realistic: This element relates to the team's capabilities. To challenge my teams, I assigned two levels of achievement for each of their major goals. Regarding the goal of revenue improvement, history shows that a 4% increase is what other teams have achieved on average. Given the history, a 4% increase is *"acceptable"* performance. Falling below 4% is not acceptable and warrants immediate improvement.

In addition to a base goal of 4% I would assign a *"stretch goal"* of perhaps a 5% improvement. If the team achieves a 5% increase in revenue, they would have exceeded their performance expectation. With a two level goal, the team has a good chance of meeting their goals and at the same time, with extraordinary effort, may be able to exceed their objectives.

I've worked with managers (lets call them "Boss-holes") that purposely *"test"* their people by giving them goals that are unrealistic. When the team fails to meet their objectives the Boss-hole has a reason for dismissal. At the same time there are a number of managers that assign unrealistic goals simply out of ignorance or incompetence. You should be able to discuss and explain the validity of your goals.

Timely: Timely refers to the goal's relevance rather than getting it done *"on time."* If we simply called it *Relevance* instead of timely our SMART acronym becomes SMARR and we can't have that! In order for a goal to be relevant (or timely) the results of the action should have some sort of affect on current company performance. From our prior example, increasing revenue by the fourth quarter of the current year has relevance. Assigning a goal to increase revenue by fourth quarter five years into the future is not relevant. Unless your team is creating a strategic plan, assigning goals that do not have an impact on current results is an inane waste of resources and time.

Provide resources! It is the manager's job to make sure their teams have the resources needed to accomplish their goals. The manager may assign more goals than can be done with the available resources. When this happens, either more resources are required or the project list needs prioritizing. Remember, although the best team can do anything, it can't do everything. The manager needs to either secure additional resources or re-prioritize the active projects.

The flip side of over-scheduling is not assigning enough work to keep the team busy. Believe me, a team with idle resources will be noticed. When you don't provide enough work for them, some team members may get reassigned. When you have a choice, it is better to over-assign work and set priorities than it is to under-assign work and lose resources.

Resource balancing: Some projects are "self contained" and can be completed without help from other groups. However, many projects require specialized input from other teams. One of the more difficult aspects of resource planning is to balance the workload of everyone involved in the project, especially those "outside of" your direct control. Those "outside" groups you will rely on will be scheduled working on projects for other teams as well as yours. Coordination of cross-functional resources, especially when plans change, quickly becomes very complex and costly.

Resource balancing seems like a simple problem to solve with some sort of high-level mathematical algorithm. The good news is that there are a number of software companies selling resource-planning software. They work well on those simple self-contained projects; but so would an Excel spreadsheet. The bad news is I have not seen a resource management tool that addresses the complexities of cross-functional resource planning and re-planning. The following example shows how a simple project quickly goes awry when it is stricken by unforeseen delays and scheduling constraints.

> Assume you manage an IT development team tasked with building a computer program. Best estimates indicate it will take your team 100 person days to design, code, test and install the software. The project also requires resource time from other teams. Five days from the infrastructure team

and ten days from the database team. The easy calculation is that this project will require a total of 115 person days of work. At $30/hr. the estimated cost of the project is $27,600 assuming an 8-hour workday and no overtime.

What follows is a detailed work plan identifying start dates; time required; and planned completion dates for the various steps in the project. You feel pretty confident with this plan. In fact, this plan has been entered into your new resource planning software. Life is good…

> Design and coding work by your team will take 55 days starting on April 20 and completed on June 15.
>
> On June 15 the infrastructure team will join your folks to do their 5 days of work.
>
> Once the infrastructure work is complete on June 20th, your team has 25 days of coding to complete by July 15th.
>
> The database resources join your team on July 15th for their 10 days of work to be completed on July 25th.
>
> Your team needs 5 more days to complete the project and install it on August 1 at a cost of $27,600.

Life *was* good. Now reality happens:

> Your team experiences a 2-day delay in design work followed by a 5-day coding delay. Cost: $1,680.
>
> The Infrastructure team must wait until coding is done. The earliest they could have started was June 22nd but due to other commitments they cannot get to your project until July 5th. They must complete their tasks before your team can start coding again on July 10th. Your team must eat the 15-day delay. Cost: $3,600.
>
> The database team was schedule to start on your project July 15th but your team needs 25 days to code once the infrastructure work is complete. The database team is idle

for 25 days until this coding is completed on Aug 10. Your project is charged for their 25-day delay. Cost: $6,000.

Due to other scheduled commitments, the database team will not be available for 15 more days. Your team is idle for these 15 days. Cost: $3,600.

The database work is finally complete on Sept 5th. Your team needs 5 more days to wrap up the project and install it on Sept 10th.

Six weeks late and 50% over budget!

What was the fatal flaw in the plan? The flaw was to assume that resources would be available precisely when *your* project needed them. Just like you, the managers of the infrastructure and database teams are under cost pressures to fully utilize their resources. They pre-schedule them on other projects to assure their dance card is full. They can't be allowed to sit idle *just in case* your project slips its dates. As a result, your project is six weeks late with a 50% cost overrun of nearly $15,000. This was a very simple project. Planning constraints explain why IT projects are frequently late and usually over budget

The initial resource plan for cross-functional work is easy to create. However, when the plan experiences any sort of delay, and plans always experience delays, it becomes extremely difficult to re-plan and re-balance all of the resources in real time without a negative impact. Delays and scheduling issues become magnified. Cross-functional resource scheduling and complexities caused by delays are the primary reason why projects take more time and cost more money than initially expected.

It is logical to make sure resources and funding have been secured before starting a project. However, there are other *less obvious* ways the manager can help in order to eliminate issues down the road.

For example:

Goal alignment: The goals assigned to your staff should be aligned with the overall goals of the firm. If not, your team is going to hit roadblock after roadblock as they attempt to engage other teams whose goals are not aligned.

Peer-to-peer relationships: Initiate relationship building with all of the teams your group will work with. Junior staff, especially when new to the firm, will need help establishing linkages. Paving this road improves the chance for success.

Manage up: Make sure upper management is both aware of and supportive of what your people are trying to achieve. Nothing helps your team more than an endorsement from the CEO. It gives instant credibility.

Be available: Make yourself available to offer your expertise when needed to resolve roadblocks. Although tempting, be careful not to mettle in the process. Knowing when to engage and provide advice comes with experience.

Get out of the way? I'm their manager – shouldn't I be involved? It sounds simple but this is a difficult skill for managers to learn. They believe they should be involved in every step their people take, demanding to see every excruciating detail. This is called *"micro managing."* This type of close oversight conveys a message that the team is not trusted to achieve results without you. It may also signal an insecure manager; one who is not comfortable letting his or her team go on its own. A good analogy is teaching a child to ride a two-wheeler. They start with training wheels. Then, Mom or Dad runs behind the bike while the child is gaining confidence. Eventually, however, Mom or Dad needs to let go.

Managing with Statistical Process Control

Instead of micro managing your team, a routine review of results using Statistical Process Control might be a better alternative. As its name implies, this technique uses statistical tools to measure and track results. The data is reviewed to see if the process is operating *"in control"* or not. Statistical Process Control is nothing more than measuring, recording and reviewing process results. There is no need to take action until an individual measure falls outside the process control limits. Control limits are set at plus or minus 3 standard deviations from the mean and 98% of all values will fall within the upper and lower control values.

The first step is to identify key process parameters that can affect results. For example, one process requirement may be to heat treat an item at 500 degrees (plus or minus 50) for fifteen minutes. This step is critical in achieving the desired quality level. Therefore, a critical element is oven heat. The operator is instructed to measure and record the temperature of the oven each hour. These measures are then displayed on a run chart. The horizontal axis is time and the vertical axis is temperature. The run chart will look similar to the following.

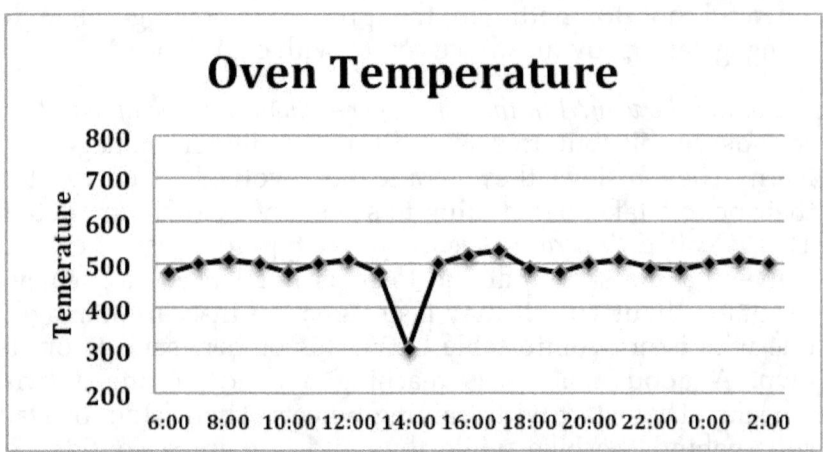

If temperature readings are in the acceptable range of 500 plus or minus 50 degrees, there is no need to adjust the dials. The readings represent normal process variation. This is a key concept that applies to all Statistical Process Control charts.

However, the 300-degree reading at 14:00 is well outside the acceptable range. The manager should ask the team to explain the set of conditions that caused this observation to be *"out of control"* and the actions taken to prevent a recurrence.

Service Level Agreements (SLA's) are performance targets that are agreed to by all parties. Tracking SLA's will indicate how well we are able to satisfy our customers. An example might be, "95% of all outstanding bills will be paid within ten days of receipt." Another might be, "90% of all new work requests will have estimates created within 48 hours." SLA results can also be displayed using Statistical Process Control run charts to facilitate a quick and easy review of key results.

Instead of micro managing, consider using Statistical Process Control to review process performance. In this way the manager can be confident the team is effectively achieving their objectives and taking steps to address out-of-control situations. Reviews can be set up on a daily, weekly, monthly or quarterly pacing; whatever makes sense. It is appropriate to ask your team to notify you when they experience incidents they cannot rectify on their own. Being made aware of these ahead of time allows the manager to work with his or her peers to avert major problems.

Things managers should not do

Fraternization: It may be acceptable to establish a friendly relationship with your staff; i.e. joining them for a beer after work to celebrate accomplishments. It is one thing to be friendly but another to be friends. Becoming friends may put you in a position to choose between loyalty to your company or your friends. The trust the company has placed in you will be lost if tactical plans fall into the wrong hands. Becoming friends with your staff jeopardizes your ability to discipline them. If it will be difficult to fire your best friend, don't allow anyone on your staff to become a best friend.

> *Side note:* Managing a workgroup you were once part of is a difficult transition. Going from *"one of the guys"* to *"leader of the pack"* requires new relationships with former peers. You have to set the ground rules early. Make sure they know

that you were chosen to lead the group and share your expectations with them. Then just follow the mantra: set goals, provide resources and get out of the way.

Favoritism undermines one's ability to manage the team. The staff knows when certain individuals receive more attention than others. This can start innocently when star performers become your *"go to"* people because they are reliable. Try to give everyone the same opportunities, and reward them equitably as warranted by their performance.

Empty promises are best left to the politicians. When you make a promise you cannot keep (whether intended or not) it kills credibility with your staff. Once your credibility is gone, losing the trust your folks placed in you is close behind. Without trust, you become just another ineffective empty suit.

Abusive or fowl language has no place in the workplace. Sure there are some folks that will not be offended, or at least act like they are not. But why risk it? Whenever you open your mouth, expect that what you say and words you used will be recorded and replayed over and over. This is another one of those things I am better at preaching than practicing.

Harassment of any kind is never acceptable. There are many types of harassment: sexual (it goes both ways ladies and gentlemen); age; physical disabilities; sexual orientation, racial; political affiliation; religious; etc. Harassment is using one's position-power to negatively affect another's ability to freely function in the workplace. Harassment comes in many shapes and sizes. Sometimes it is blatant such as groping someone in exchange for a promotion. It can also be subtle, such as the ridicule received when traveling with an opposite sex colleague. If that ridicule *"shames"* you into not utilizing or promoting a capable person, you are using your position to affect their *ability* to freely function without prejudice.

Blame someone else? Avoid the temptation to blame someone else when things don't go according to plan or when bad news needs to be presented. It is very easy to blame the guy who came before you when things go wrong, but that is the coward's way out. Few people really care how you feel on a certain issue or who is to blame. What they want to know is how you are planning to deal with it. Stand tall and accept the responsibilities that come with your position. Take ownership of the decisions handed down from above. Your crew will appreciate the truth and will rally to support you when you need it.

Public flogging went out with the plague during the dark ages. Yes, discipline is needed from time to time but it is best done behind closed doors. Nothing is more brutal to an ego than being chewed out in public, especially in front of co-workers. This is usually done in the *"heat of the moment"* when tempers are flaring. It is best to wait until you have calmed down before confronting a problem employee. This is another thing I am better at preaching than practicing.

Lying is another activity best reserved for politicians. The thing about lying is that eventually the truth will come out and when it does, your credibility suffers. The big problem with lying is trying to remember all of the lies that cascade one after the other. Once you start, it is difficult to stop. The truth is far easier to remember. Try it.

Farting in meetings is never appreciated. Have you noticed that every so often someone expresses something rather foul in a meeting? I am referring to complaining or whining about something totally beyond the control of those in the meeting. (What did you think I meant?) The negative feelings, and subsequent rant, build until finally, they can no longer be contained. The dinge of negativity quickly spreads across the room. It will derail positive thoughts and ideas and may eventually cloud the reason for having met in the first place. The impact is much worse when the boss is the perpetrator. Of course, I am using the term *"farting"* metaphorically. Farting in a meeting would be cruel if there is no easy escape.

Bad mouthing other teams, peers or your boss will never lead to anything good. Sure, it allows you to let off steam but the best that can happen is that nothing changes. On the other hand, those you are speaking poorly of will eventually learn of your disdain, as nothing stays private. Using social media to spew your poison is infinitely stupid. Remember, once it is posted it is out there forever. Enough said!

Things managers should do more of:

Give praise to your people for their accomplishments. Do this in a sincere way or don't do it at all. Phony praise damages your credibility and well, makes you look like an idiot. It will also diminish your ability to manage the staff. The degree of praise should be proportional to the importance of the actual accomplishment.

Balance responsibility and authority. Nothing is worse than having responsibility for an outcome without having the authority to affect it. It is like expecting someone to coach a team and win games without having the ability to decide who plays and who sits on the bench. Responsibility without authority creates frustration and leads to major problems.

Keep your teams informed of everything they need to know in order to effectively execute their job. Sure, depending on the level of the manager, certain things are not to be shared and must remain confidential. It is not always obvious to people what is "OK" to share and what is not. This will come with experience. When in doubt, ask your boss before you spill the beans.

Maintaining positive energy is surprisingly powerful. Teams reflect the leader's mood. When you are upbeat, so are they. At the risk of over using sports analogies, the often-used term *"momentum shift"* describes a swing from average performance to a level that achieves superior results.

An impressive momentum shift occurred during a football game between Dallas and Green Bay on December 15, 2013 in Dallas. The Packers quarterback, Aaron Rodgers, broke his collarbone six weeks earlier and was not cleared to play.

Green Bay's record during his absence was just 1-5. Reserve quarterback, Matt Flynn, and the Packer's were embarrassed on both sides of the ball in the first half of the game. They managed just 120 yards of offense. The defense gave up 26 points. The Cowboys led 26 – 3 at the half. Something happened in both locker rooms during halftime. Somehow the momentum changed when the teams came out to play the second half. The Packers, scoring five touchdowns, overcame a huge deficit to beat the Cowboys by a final score of 37 – 36! This is a great example of how positive energy changed the mood of the team and the outcome of the game.

Marketing your staff does two things. First, it keeps the organization informed about what they are working on. Second, it's a good way to solicit the support they may need from other parts of the organization. When people don't know what your group is doing, negative feelings may develop. We are naturally negative about things we don't understand. This lack of understanding can frequently lead to stereotypes, prejudice and decisions based on faulty assumptions.

I am amazed at how easily the leadership of an organization can be swayed by well-marketed ideas; even the dopiest ones. The best way to get stakeholders on board is to pre-sell your ideas to them face-to-face, one at a time. This is called *"greasing the skids"* and it is a great way to build consensus.

Performance reviews should be done on a routine basis. People want to know how they are doing. They want to be told what they are doing right as well as what they are doing wrong. Praise is a powerful motivator and can be gratifying when it comes from the boss. People don't wake up in the morning looking forward to going to work and screwing something up. If they are not performing properly the boss needs to tell them. Giving constructive feedback is a great skill for new managers to learn and exercise.

I want to be president! Formal performance reviews should always include a discussion about the employee's career aspirations. Regardless of their goals, even if it is to become president of the firm, the manager's job is to coach their staff on how to achieve their goals; including becoming president. Never tell someone they are not capable of achieving what it is they aspire to be. Instead, help them plan their career path by explaining what they need to do in order to achieve their dreams.

Disciplinary action, if not administered consistently, will result in a collapse of trust and respect for the manager. Integrity suffers along with a degradation of team dynamics. When the manager shows preferential treatment, team relationships are damaged. Without trust in each other, the team will not be capable of performing at a high level. Trust is very easy to destroy and very difficult to restore.

Giving bad news is something every manager will face in his or her career. It is best done in a straightforward manner. Layoffs, demotions, organization changes, etc. happen from time to time. It is imperative that the manager delivers bad news directly and avoids delegating this task to someone else. However, if the news will significantly change the lifestyle of the employee (i.e. a layoff) make sure an H.R. representative is present. Together, the direct manager and H.R. person will be able to address the many questions that might come up.

Years ago I worked for a wonderful manager named Clarence. He was bright, witty and bald. There was not a single strand of hair on his head. One day I asked him how he became bald. He answered, "If you ever get the chance to manage others, you will find out!" We will hear more about Clarence later.

Chapter 8: Managing Projects

The five essential steps of project management

The typical project has five distinct phases or steps associated with it that are independent from the output the project will deliver. Whether launching a new product, creating a new computer program, or constructing a building, the overall structure of these projects is the same. This allows us to teach Project Management as an academic discipline. The essential phases found in every project are *Defining, Planning, Executing, Monitoring, and Closing Out.*

A combination of *Product* knowledge and *Project* knowledge are required to complete most projects. Product knowledge is that which is specific to the output of the project itself. For example, if we are building a new computer program, knowledge of IT is required. If we are building a new office building, construction skills are critical. Project knowledge, on the other hand, pertains to managing the flow of the project itself. Project management skills are universal and there are courses that teach these skills. Individuals with project management skills can manage a wide variety of projects.

Finding the ideal project manager, proficient in both process and product knowledge, is difficult. Project management is a teachable skill. It is common for firms to invest in training employees with strong product knowledge on the finer points of managing projects. There are a number of excellent project management training programs available on the market. Many will offer certification. I found it was easier to teach a product expert to become a project manager than it was to teach a project manager to become a product expert.

Problem definition

The very first step is to define the problem that needs to be solved. Nothing else makes sense until this is done. The project manager should address these basic questions:

What is the client's objective? If constructing an office building, the project manager needs to know: How many private offices and conference rooms are needed? How much space is needed for public areas? What is the intended function of the building? Will there need to be space allocated for a dining facility, retail shops, etc.? If creating a new computer program, the project manager needs to know how will it change the way the user does their job. If designing a new product, the project manager needs to ask how the consumer will use this product. Are there special considerations for shipping and handling that may need to be addressed as well?

Does it fit the corporate strategy? If the project doesn't fit the overarching objectives of the firm, it will face an uphill battle from the beginning. Your project is dead in the water if upper management does not support it. Here's what happens: Your project may require input from other groups that have to account for where they spend their time. If not approved, they will be reluctant to work on your project because they will not get funding! Non-sanctioned projects, regardless of their value, will not be supported.

How will you know when you get there? The project manager and client need to define what the successful outcome of the project is and how to measure it. These metrics should reflect the requirements that were defined for the project. For example, if the primary objective were to increase worker productivity, perhaps a measure of *"units produced per hour"* is appropriate. It is important to understand current baseline performance data in order to compare the results both before and after the project. Sometimes there may be multiple changes in play that could cloud our ability to accurately measure results.

What are the solution options? Define the range of options the project manager may consider in order to solve the problem. For example, can we build a new office building from ground up or should we focus on renovating an existing space? Are there certain geographies that should not be considered for locating the new plant? Should we purchase new software or modify existing code in order to provide the functionality required by the user?

What are the benefits? The client should be able to describe, in detail, the tangible benefits the project will deliver. This includes describing *"how"* benefits will be generated and validated post install. One of my hot buttons are *"savings"* that are associated with reducing labor hours. For example, "This project will improve labor efficiency saving $520,000 per year." This is easy to say but difficult to prove. Without validation it becomes a game of *"Liar's Poker"* with the best liar getting their project approved. When pressed for the details about where the $520,000 will come from, you might get an answer such as: "We will save 4 hours per person per week. With 100 employees it saves 400 labor hours each week. Since the average cost per employee is $25/hour the resulting savings amounts to $10,000 per week or $520,000 per year."

The reality about cost savings based on labor savings is that the labor cost doesn't go down until someone comes off the payroll. Until there are names identified that will be eliminated, there can be no savings. You will often hear the argument that even though nobody is eliminated, each person will have more time to focus on work. In our example, each person has 4 additional hours of free time every week and could use it to increase output. I can buy the argument as long as there is a way to measure the associated productivity increase.

As I think back on my years working on projects associated with labor savings, by this point in time, with all the savings added up, there should be no people left!

Create a written project proposal. It is a good idea to document all of the discussions and agreements reached during the project definition phase. They become the basis for a formal proposal to be shared with upper management and key stakeholders to help them understand the project. If they don't understand the project it will be difficult to secure funding as well as the approval to proceed.

Plan the work

Once the proposal is complete and approved, the next step is to create the project plan. The plan includes the project's scope; a list of participants and their specific responsibilities; communication strategies; risk management; key milestones; budgets; and an implementation strategy.

Managing Scope Creep. The project's scope defines the expected results, project specifications and the tasks needed to deliver them. It drives the materials and labor cost required to solve the problem. Every project experiences changes to the original proposal. Typically, the client tends to add things to the final product but rarely are elements eliminated. This is known as *"scope creep."*

As things change, it is important to keep track of them and update the proposal. Show the initial points and all of the changes to them so a comparison to the original agreement can be made. Capture the incremental cost; functionality changes; and time required to complete the project every time the scope changes. This is where the project manager earns his or her pay. The client needs to understand that scope changes have an associated cost. Make sure the client signs off on all scope changes.

Create the project team: Projects don't complete themselves. A project team needs to be identified as early as possible, (I know this sounds stupid) well before the project starts! I've seen projects start up without identifying the team first. This leads to confusion and ultimately a great deal of rework once the permanent team is named.

It takes some time for resources to get into the flow of the project. Often, upper management mistakenly thinks that a warm body automatically qualifies as a project resource. They forget that warm bodies must first go through a learning curve before they can be useful on the project.

Team size will be determined by the size and complexity of the project. A large team will need a leadership structure with specific names assigned to key responsibilities. For example, who will lead the project? Who will be the client liaisons? Who will manage potential technology changes? The team leadership resources are often overlooked and not incorporated into the resource plan.

Project Communications: Keep the organization up-to-speed on the status of your project. The frequency and protocols of your posting will be based on the size of the project and organizational practices. Whatever fits the organization is fine except for NOT delivering a routine update, that is not fine. Make sure your up-line management is aware when major issues arise, especially if they are beyond your ability to resolve them.

Risk management: Provide a perspective on potential risks associated with the project. Identify what may go wrong and what can be done to minimize and recover from the damage. It is wise to do this proactively, before someone asks about it. When you raise the concern, it helps to defuse the negative reactions. It is best to show you have thought it through ahead of time instead of merely reacting to it.

Key milestones: The project plan identifies specific dates to complete milestones. A project *"whip"* is often used to keep an eye on how the project is progressing against those key milestones. The whip will develop a feel for how things are going and can predict when delays may occur without some sort of intervention taking place.

The budget: Projects generally have 2 funding components; one is capital, the other is expense. Capital spending is generally for items used in the production of income that have a life of more than one year. This includes machinery, equipment, buildings, vehicles, etc. Capital spending is amortized over the life of the asset. A piece of machinery that cost $10,000 with a life expectancy of five years creates depreciation of $2,000 per year to offset income. The other component of the budget is expense. Expense is consumed within the year it was spent. Typical expense items include fuel, utilities, office supplies, etc.

Experienced project managers know that every project will encounter unexpected events that will alter the plan. These *"alterations"* almost always have a negative impact on the project's budget. A contingency fund, say 10% to 20% of the project's initial estimate, is incorporated into the budget. The project manager is allowed some flexibility to overspend the base budget but must attain approval if the project cost is expected to exceed the base plus contingency.

Implementation strategy: A good deal of thought needs to be given to the project's implementation strategy. Installation and implementation are used interchangeably but actually mean different things. Installation refers to the actions required for the project to *"go live"* and be available for the client to use. Implementation refers to the preparation and training of the user so they can manage the functionality and begin generating benefits associated with the project. Installation and implementation are often planned jointly. This assures that when the project goes live, the users are ready and able to quickly work through the learning curve and deliver the benefits as planned.

> *When?* The first question to answer regarding installation is *"when."* Try to avoid points in time when resources will be focused on competing events. For example, in retail we never went live with any new computer system at the end of a quarter. There are many activities that need to be done with financial reporting at quarter end. Also, customer demand tends to increase at that time.

How? How your project will be installed needs to be well planned too. If the project involves building a new warehouse, someone needs to manage the cutover from the old warehouse to the new. They need to make sure equipment is ready; staff is trained; inventory is available and orders start flowing to the new warehouse.

Who? Who will be affected by the project and how will their role change once it is installed? Someone needs to be responsible for training the users and explain how the project will change the way they do their work. The client often does this task. There may be a number of other roles (from security guards to the facility manager) that could be affected by the project. Include them in the planning.

Where? The project may be a new computer system that may eventually be deployed across the globe. Will it be rolled out to all locations at the same time? Or, will it be a series of country-by-country rollouts?

Work the plan

Executing the plan results in completing the work needed to deliver the project's requirements. The project team is fully engaged and carries most of the load during this stage. The project manager is engaged and will manage the following topics and issues associated with them.

Scope: The project is completed on time based on the most recent approved scope. Resources with requisite skills are on the job to deliver the work. All approved scope changes should become part of the revised project scope.

Budget: Manage the budget for labor and materials required to complete the work. The organization is posted when actual spending varies from plan.

Risks: Project risks should be identified in the planning phase. However, new risks may arise during execution and all stakeholders should be made aware of them.

Communication: Assemble and routinely present milestone status, project parameters, and any open issues affecting the delivery of the project.

A milestone is an activity that is to be accomplished by a certain date. A parameter is a guideline (i.e. spending) defining the bounds of the project.

I prefer to present open issues in a table that contains: a brief description of the issue; the name the individual responsible for resolving it; the date it will be resolved.

Keeping the project moving: Often, the project experiences unforeseen events. *"Breakdowns"* or *"roadblocks"* by their very nature are never predicted during the planning phase. If they were, they could be resolved before they occur. A roadblock can easily affect the viability of the project as well as the mindset and demeanor of the project team. Once the team senses the project is threatened, they may feel beaten and give up. When roadblocks occur, the project manager must apply his or her leadership skills and create a change in mood and direction to assure the project survives.

The typical response when faced with a roadblock is to change objectives instead of removing the roadblock. Think of the project as a 3-legged stool with one leg being cost, the second quality and the third time. By changing objectives, a breakdown affecting one of these legs is solved by adjusting the other two. For example, if a breakdown will cause the project to be delivered late, the response is to get the project back on track by either cutting quality (i.e. functionality) or spending more money or both. So old school! The savvy project manager, trained in managing breakdowns, will use the team to brainstorm a creative way solution to remove the roadblock WITHOUT affecting any of the other legs on the stool.

There is an entire segment of project management dedicated to helping teams effectively resolve breakdowns when they occur. Rest assured, they will occur. There are a number of firms that can help your team establish processes to search for and identify creative solutions when breakdowns occur. I have personally used the services of one of these firms and am thankful I did. The ability to manage breakdowns is very important when managing large, complex projects.

To understand the essence of managing breakdowns, we must first become comfortable with the three *"worlds"* of knowledge: The *"World We Know"* the *"World We Know We Don't Know"* and the *"World We Didn't Know We Didn't Know."* Confused? Let me explain.

> *The World We Know* is all of the knowledge we have been accumulating since recorded history began. Think of it as everything known about a certain topic. For example, we know that if we drop something, the Earth's gravity will pull it to the ground with the same force as any other item. We believe this because we observe it every time.
>
> *The World We Know We Don't Know* is a body of knowledge we are sure we don't know. For example, we know there is nothing immune to Earth's gravity. We know this since we have yet to identify anything that defies gravity.
>
> *The World We Didn't Know We Didn't Know* is the body of knowledge yet to be revealed. This is the world where discovery and innovation come from. We discussed how paradigms blind us. The content of the *World We Didn't Know We Didn't Know* is often the very knowledge our paradigms keep us from seeing. Man could not imagine a way to escape Earth's gravity. That is until jet propulsion was discovered! Don't give up…the answer is out there.

Post mortem: Maintaining a *"lessons learned"* journal is a good way to document issues encountered during the project. When collected and published they can be made available to help future project teams avoid making similar mistakes. These also become invaluable tools to accelerate the training of new project teams and enable them to get up-to-speed quickly.

Monitor progress

The flow master: There are two key aspects of every project that should be monitored. The first is the on-time completion of the many milestones or sub-tasks. This is done to assure the viability of the timetable and ultimately the project's target end-date. When dates start to slip, even for seemingly minor issues, the on-time completion of the project is at risk. The second aspect is the consumption of key resources (materials, labor and capital) versus the pace assumed in the project plan and budget. Monitoring these two elements will provide the project manager with the ability to predict issues ahead of time, allowing the opportunity to rectify them in a proactive manner. Large complex projects will benefit from assigning an individual dedicated to monitoring these.

> One of the larger, more complex projects I managed was comprised of hundreds of individual tasks that each had to be completed in order for the overall project to *"go live"* at the predetermined date. This date was not negotiable! I was fortunate to have Bill monitoring the workflow of the project. At the end of each day, Bill would communicate with each of the project leads to make sure their activities for that day were completed as planned. If for some reason they were not, Bill would reschedule them in order to keep the final delivery date in tact. With Bill's input and the dedication of the team, we were able to deliver the project as designed, on time and within budget. Thanks Bill!

Project close out

Once the project is complete, a formal closeout is conducted. The closeout is when the project team and the client officially agree that the scope of the project has been completed to the client's satisfaction. It is the vehicle with which to notify the organization that the project is finished, the project team will be redeployed to other projects and funding stops. Once the closeout is complete, no additional work can be done to the project without incremental funding.

Acknowledgement: The project team and client acknowledge that the project was delivered as defined in the proposal. This is when that written proposal becomes important. It is a contract of sorts and will help defuse arguments down the road. The client and project leaders literally sit down together going over the key deliverables to make sure they are complete. If the project was planned and monitored properly there will be few surprises at this point.

Punch list items: It is not unusual for minor issues to arise that need to be rectified before the project can officially be deemed complete. The project team and client will create a punch list of these issues along with a plan to address them. The punch list items are usually small technical issues that need to be resolved before the project is able to deliver its benefits. They typically require a minimal amount of effort to resolve. A word of caution: make sure the punch list does not become a way to add functionality or correct design flaws overlooked when the project proposal was drafted. Once the punch list items are complete, all further work requires a new proposal and incremental funding.

Documentation: When the project is complete, it is not over until the team archives all the necessary project files and documents lessons learned. Documentation is often done haphazardly and is rarely given the priority it deserves. Teams change and people move on. When modifications are needed in the future, the next project team will not have a clue about what was done or why it was done without solid documentation. The project management circle is not complete until the documentation is done.

Project management can be very rewarding. It challenges one's creative side; helps to sharpen leadership skills; and affords the manager a great deal of visibility.

Chapter 9: Leading and Leadership

In Chapter 7 we discussed *"managing others"* with a focus on effective utilization of the firm's primary resources: people, materials and processes. *"Managing"* assures processes are completed as designed to produce the desired product or output. The enterprising manager also seeks ways to improve *"how"* those processes are done. The manager prioritizes activities, sets goals, assigns work and maintains a fiduciary responsibility to the firm. In addition to monitoring activities to assure plans are met, he or she must mesh the varied personalities and egos of the people actually doing the work.

Leadership on the other hand is creating a vision of the future and motivating the entire team to get there. In this chapter we will dissect the various aspects of leadership to better understand exactly what it is, the role it plays in the workplace, and how we learn to lead. We will also discuss what happens when leadership is missing from the equation.

<u>What is leadership?</u>

Most definitions of leadership are similar. I happen to like the following: *Leadership is simply a process of social influence in which one person can enlist the aid and support of others in the accomplishment of a common task.* Every definition of leadership reinforces the notion that a leader is an individual, NOT a team. Sure, you can probably name a number of leadership teams. They are typically comprised of the firm's top managers who act in an advisory role to assure activities are aligned, and reinforce the strategic direction of the firm. We will review a list of famous leaders. Sadly, I could not find a famous *"leadership team"* to include on the list.

Famous leaders: In order to better understand what leadership is, we will first examine the common traits of well-known leaders throughout history.

Jesus Christ: This man was able to mobilize a tremendous following, *Christians*. According to Pew Research, Christians currently comprise about a third of all people on earth. This percentage has been virtually unchanged for the past one hundred years – 35% in 1910 and 32% in 2010.

Attila the Hun: Mr. Hun was able to shape a wandering band of mercenary tribal nomads into undisputed rulers of the ancient world. There have been many books written about Attila the Hun and his win-directed, take-charge style of management. I think I worked for his great grandson once.

Adolph Hitler: Steadfast in his belief that descendants of the Germanic race were without equal, it took only three years to convince an entire country to follow him; without the Internet! The Holocaust he launched resulted in the mass genocide of approximately six million Jews during World War II. Imagine what a narcissistic bastard can do today.

Sir Winston Churchill: "Winnie" was the Prime Minister of Great Britain from 1940 to 1945 and again from 1951 to 1955. Widely regarded as one of the greatest wartime leaders of the 20th century, Churchill mobilized the allies to defeat Hitler's reign of terror.

Margaret Thatcher: The Iron Lady, elected to be Britain's first female Prime Minister, served from 1979 to 1991. Her conservative views led England out of years of economic and political turmoil; government bankruptcy; rising unemployment; and many violent labor union conflicts.

Mahatma Gandhi: Gandhi preached civil disobedience in order to gain India's independence from Great Britain. In August of 1947 the British Parliament voted to grant India its independence. Sadly, less than six months later, a Hindu extremist assassinated Gandhi.

Ronald Reagan: Mr. Reagan was elected as President of the United States in 1980 and served two terms. He inherited an economy in turmoil. By the middle of his first term, jobs were plentiful and the economy was growing. He helped dismantle communism and urged removing the Berlin Wall.

Indira Gandhi: This woman was India's third Prime Minister from 1966 to 1977 and was reelected again in 1980. She was responsible for creating agricultural programs, improving the lives of India's poor. Her Sikh bodyguards assassinated her in 1984. Does it seem like India needs gun control?

Osama bin laden: This man tops the evil list. He aligned Islamic terrorist groups into a global organization, Al-Qaeda. Vowing *"Jihad"* on the U.S., he planned attacks on U.S. citizens around the world including the World Trade Center, resulting in over 3,000 deaths. Thanks Seal Team 6!

Nelson Mandela: Madiba was a political activist who spent 27 years in prison (1962 to 1989). After his release he worked to peacefully free his country from years of white minority rule known as Apartheid. He was elected as President of South Africa from 1994 to 1999. He died December 5, 2013.

Common characteristics? There are other well-known leaders we could have listed, but those noted above should suffice for us to identify and discuss common leadership characteristics.

First, they are each charismatic but in different ways. Their followers are attracted to them in very large numbers.

Second, each one was able to create and lead structured organizations. Many of these organizations still exist long after their deaths.

Third, each of them communicated a clear vision to their followers. There was no doubt about what they stood for.

Finally, (and obviously) they had followers. Not mindless sheep, but people who were willing to march into hell and follow the leader anywhere.

Follow the leader

It is a given that in order for one to be a leader, one must have followers. Leadership books usually focus on leaders and, as noted above, the common traits they share. For the most part, these books ignore the very essence of what it is that *followers* are looking for. Therefore, we will take a moment to explore what followers are looking for in their leaders.

We will examine the concept of leadership from the follower's perspective. In doing so, perhaps we can help aspiring leaders understand how they need to act and what they need to provide in order to attract followers. In a September 2004 Harvard Business Review article, Michael Maccoby writes:

"Followers' motivations fall into two categories; rational and irrational. The rational ones are conscious and therefore well known. They have to do with our hopes of gaining money, status, power, or entry into a meaningful enterprise by following a great leader and our fears that we will miss out if we don't. More influential, much of the time, are the irrational motivations that lie outside the realm of our awareness and, therefore, beyond our ability to control them. For the most part, these motivations arise from the powerful images and emotions in our unconscious that we project onto our relationships with leaders."

"Sigmund Freud, the founder of psychoanalysis, was the first person to provide some explanation of a follower's unconscious motivations. After practicing psychoanalysis for a number of years, Freud was puzzled to find that his patients (who were, in a sense, his followers) kept falling in love with him. Although most of his patients were women, the same thing happened with his male patients. It is a great tribute to Freud that he realized that his patients' idealization of him couldn't be traced to his own personal qualities. Instead, he concluded, people were relating to him as if he were some important person from their past; usually a parent. In undergoing therapy, or in falling in love for that matter, people were transferring experiences and emotions from past relationships onto the present. Freud thought the phenomenon was universal. He wrote, 'There is no love that does not reproduce infantile stereotypes,' which, for him, explained why so many of us choose spouses like our parents."

Freud called this phenomenon *"transference"* and theorized that our relationships with leaders are based on stereotypes formed early in life. Are we attracted to (or repulsed by) our leaders because we subconsciously transfer the relationship we had with our parents to our leaders? Who knows? Then again, Freud enjoyed cigars, often smoking up to 20 per day! What do you suppose he would say about that?

Staying within the *"Winning in the Workplace"* theme, here are some traits followers look for in their workplace leaders.

Independent thinking. We want leaders with the ability to *"think outside the box"* with a mind of their own. They are not afraid to offer opinions and new ideas, even if they happen to be contrary to the status quo.

Ability to lead us to new places. We want our leaders to take us to places we would not have gone to on our own. They are visionaries but also demonstrate the ability to achieve their vision. Good leaders rely on peripheral vision to identify when it is time to change course or take corrective action. When we look back at our career path, we can see how good leaders influenced and shaped our journey.

Self Confidence. We want to follow someone who is self assured in his or her abilities. Nothing diminishes the confidence in our leaders more than when they need to ask permission! A leader who demands the team asks permission before taking any action is stifling. The leader should build confidence in the team's ability to make sound decisions by describing the *"boundaries"* within which the staff can make decisions. As staff confidence, capability and knowledge grows, so will the boundaries.

Integrity. We follow someone we can be proud of and who is respected by his or her peers. We want to look up to our leaders, not look down on them. When leaders bend or disregard established rules, their organization will do the same. Soon, anarchy follows.

> It is important to note that integrity is defined within the follower's frame of reference; a more global court may not agree. This may explain why Hitler's following grew in Germany, while the rest of the world saw his evil.

Emotional control. There is plenty of drama in our world today. We want leaders to be calm and collected. Flying off with rants, cursing, and emotional outbursts concerns us. We want to be able to approach the leader with issues and not worry whether he or she will come unglued.

Caring. We want our leaders to show empathy when certain events impact our personal lives. Our families are an integral part of each of us. They are the reason we put up with workplace frustrations. It is comforting when our leaders understand and care about us on a human level.

Provide honest feedback. We want to know where we stand and how to improve performance. Many firms require a formal feedback session every six months or so. How stupid! Leaders should not wait for a formal review to offer feedback. Praising good efforts and pointing out mistakes should happen spontaneously. A good leader is committed to helping team members develop to the full extent of their capabilities. Constructive criticism, offered when needed, will help employees grow personally and professionally.

Humility. Good leaders are willing to receive feedback from employees at all levels of the organization. Those closest to the process (i.e. their staff) often see things through a lens the leader doesn't have. Encouraging open feedback will provide new perspectives resulting in a better solution. Good leaders are able to balance confidence and humility.

Results oriented: Leaders are winners who produce results. Their personal commitment extends well beyond their role and personal success. Their legacy is to be known as the person who left a lasting handprint on the firm's results. They are also remembered for how they cared about their people and the positive (or negative) impact on their lives.

It is great to have leaders whose leadership style impacts you in such a way that you would utter this phrase, "I Will Follow That Leader Anywhere!" That is the power of followers.

The role of leadership

Without a destination in mind, any path will take you there! The most important role of the leader is to develop a future vision for their organization. Leaders at the very top of the house are looked to for strategic vision. However, each department within the organization should also have a vision linking them to the overarching direction of the company. In general terms, the leader's vision helps align all resources so they can march with a common purpose and endpoint in mind.

A good vision contains many of the following properties:

A mental picture: A vision should provide a mental picture of what *"future state"* looks like. A clear picture allows us to visualize goals and create plans to achieve them.

Idealistic and realistic: Although it may sound contrary, a good vision should be both idealistic and realistic. The vision has to be realistic (achievable) so people can become engaged in it. Few of us want to spend time working on something that cannot succeed. Idealistic goals require reaching new heights that generate pride once achieved.

A good fit: A vision needs to fit within the organization's existing values, culture and environment it operates in. A food company with a vision to move into electronics is not a good fit. Identify what your organization does well and focus energy towards doing more of that.

Inspiring: A good vision must inspire people within the organization to stay focused and energized in order to reach their goals. People, when inspired, will become committed to reaching new milestones and stretching to bounds they never before thought possible.

Clarity of purpose: Everyone wants to know his or her role in executing the vision. Making clear what the firm wants to achieve and what each individual's role is creates meaning in worker's lives. The paycheck is an important reason why most of us work. However, a good vision will create an attractive future for the organization and the people in it.

Ideals: A good vision propels the organization to higher levels of excellence. External evaluations of the company's products and services validate this. Peer group praise is also an indication of recognized excellence. An example is the Academy Awards. A peer group (the Academy of Motion Picture Arts and Sciences) reviews films each year and nominates the best as being eligible to receive awards.

Ambitious: A vision needs to motivate us to reach new heights. It must be extraordinary and cause an organization to stretch well beyond their comfort zones. Ambitious visions are not about *"staying the course."* They are about achieving a level of performance that was unheard of and only dreamed about...until now.

Articulated and understood: Envision the organization as a pyramid. Strategic leadership is at the top. Most of the employees occupy various levels below the leader. In order for the vision to succeed, every layer of the pyramid must understand and embrace it. I call this the *"Pyramid of Power."* The people at the top of the pyramid make million dollar decisions. However, the vast numbers of employees on the lower levels, those in direct contact with customers, make a multitude of $10,000 decisions every day. These add up to millions of dollars. If the lower levels do not fully embrace the vision, the cumulative affect of those decisions may actually erode the firm's overarching objectives.

A successful leader creates a vision for three to five years into the future. This assures actions taken today are linked with and lead to the ultimate endgame. The Long Range Plan (LRP) is the CEO's roadmap to the future. Each sub-organization across the firm must create their own mini-LRP supporting the CEO's vision. Marketing, Manufacturing, Technology, Sales, etc. will each create their own vision or LRP. It is imperative that a solid linkage of purpose exists across and between these groups. The LRP and organizational planning when done properly will motivate and energize followers. It gives a clear picture of the future for each employee and how they will benefit from it. The basic objective is simple. The LRP should energize the organization to stand up and say, "I Will Follow That Leader Anywhere!"

Learning to lead

There is no question that a college degree is important. The correlation between higher pay and a college education is just too strong. In today's world a degree is the price of admission to the workplace. The debate in my mind is not whether a degree is valuable, but whether that degree is a prerequisite to become a leader.

Can leadership be taught? This question has been debated over and over without a clear answer. Colleges across the land have developed leadership programs in hopes of attracting both students and donors. The areas open to debate:

1. Is a college education a prerequisite to become a leader?

2. What does the curricula for a leadership program include?

3. How do we test the success of leadership programs?

Is college a prerequisite? Research from Spencer Stuart (2004) indicates 97% of today's Fortune 500 CEO's have at least an undergrad degree. Does this mean college creates leaders? Or is it a reflection of our societal expectation that high school graduates should go to college and attain at least a four-year degree? The evidence may support the latter. According to a National Association of Scholars (NAS) study, from 1947 to 1995 the number of high school graduates entering college rose from 2.3 million to 14.3 million. This rate of growth is three times faster than that of the population. We want to believe college creates better, smarter, more effective leaders. Unfortunately, there is no conclusive evidence that it does.

Conventional thinking may have this backwards. Perhaps one's drive and innate intelligence (rather than a degree) are primary prerequisites to success – both in the boardroom and in the classroom. The success of Jobs, Gates, Zuckerberg, Ellison, and Dell (none hold undergrad degrees) may have resulted from a conflict with the number of hours in a day. They each had the drive and innate intelligence, but may not have had enough time to develop their dreams *and* pursue a degree. They are part of a small minority that chose the dream instead of a degree – and won!

Curricula? According to Dr. Edwin Weaver, Unique Leaders Professional Development Consultants:

> "The _business_ world does not need highly educated people guiding it. The business world needs leaders with heart. Leaders who know the hearts of those around them and can inspire them to do great things. For decades I have studied the great leaders in the military, government and business. The majority of these leaders had very little education, but they knew the hearts of those around them. They knew what was needed."

The essence of Dr. Weaver's thoughts is that a leader must learn to know the hearts of his or her followers. Developing into a leader also requires a personal transformation. One that forces us to reexamine our beliefs and assumptions about professional identity, our role, and tasks we perform with the people we work with. To successfully create leaders, the academic environment needs to offer challenging experiences to the student. The student must also be given the opportunity to evaluate conceptual frameworks.

It is difficult to replicate these experiences and conceptual frameworks on a large scale in the classroom. Opportunities do exist for students to participate in short-term (semester-long) activities designed to sharpen leadership skills. Those with inherent leadership traits will find them helpful. Along with time and experience, these programs help the student build a capacity for leadership.

Testing our ability to train leaders. If leadership can be taught, how do we test the effectiveness of this training? After all, we can test the student's proficiency in learning other subjects such as mathematics, microbiology, English literature and so on.

The hallmarks of a great leader are the ability to create and implement a successful strategic vision, and the ability to attract followers. We can teach leadership traits to prospective leaders and we can teach the mechanics of constructing a vision statement. Colleges evaluate students on a class-by-class, semester-by-semester basis. Unfortunately, it could take years for a vision to come to fruition and for a leader to amass a following. Without tools to test leadership proficiency, can we claim to have actually taught someone to become a leader?

Can a person lead and manage at the same time?

The question, "Can an individual be both a successful leader and manager?" is frequently asked. Sure, why not? In fact, it is preferred. Problems develop when different individuals are responsible for strategy and execution. Let's examine the issues that occur when these activities develop in separate heads.

> *Strategy.* The person responsible for creating the firm's strategy does just that. A strategy is created *that someone else implements*. Then what? Since their role is to create strategies, they create additional new ones or revise existing ones in order to maintain their job. The *"strategy of the month club"* approach puts a burden on resources and confuses the organization. The *"blue sky"* guys (strategic thinkers) have

no skin in the game. If their strategy doesn't work, they will be quick to lay blame on the execution team.

Execution. The manager is responsible for execution and literally has minimal input in creating the strategic plan. The manager's role is aligning resources to implement the plan. Every time the strategy changes, the manager must revamp his or her execution approach. This is disruptive; especially if the strategy doesn't respect the impact it may have on how the work is done in a specific function.

Hybrid. Work flows more smoothly if the person creating strategy is also the one executing it. Someone that works with the team every day can develop a better perspective on what should change and how best to change it. This is much harder for someone not closely involved.

Can an organization exist without leaders?

Evolutionary vs. revolutionary change! If the firm lumbers along doing what it has always done, it is possible to continue their existence for some time without a leader. The organization cruises along, slowly *evolving* to changes in the marketplace. This is a common approach often used on mature processes and product lines. A mature product line or *"cash cow"* has limited (if any) growth potential and although profitable, slowly loses ground over time. Firms do not generally invest large sums of capital in their cash cows, preferring instead to milk them for as long as they can. The cash thrown off is used to fund other initiatives. Eventually the cash cow will die and the competition will feast on its carcass.

Leadership, on the other hand, creates revolutionary change. It shakes the very core and soul of the organization. It keeps the firm vital and moving forward. Good leaders constantly scan the environment looking for new technologies to adopt and new directions to follow. Successful leaders are always on alert to keep the firm from falling prey to unforeseen shifts in existing paradigms.

Chapter 10: Managing Your Career

Where are you headed? (Career-wise)

Earlier in this book we went to great lengths describing what a job is, how it fits into the overarching structure of the organization and how it is valued. A job, in itself, is not a career, but what one is doing at a point in time. Your career is the culmination of a number of jobs. Your career defines you in the workplace and distinguishes you among your peers. A *career path* is a sequence of jobs that add new dimensions to your skills inventory.

When planning your career, there are two important concepts to grasp. The first is creating personal goals, sort of a *"where are you going?"* proposition. The second is to find a mentor that can help you navigate through the maize of risks and opportunities you will face. Mentors are people who have *"been there"* and understand what you need to achieve your career goals. Hopefully, you will find many mentors over the course of your career.

Most people would not be content doing the same job for 30 plus years. However, those that do stay for life do so for a number of reasons. They have become comfortable with job duties, benefits, income security, aversion to risk, etc. The majority of us live paycheck-to-paycheck with every penny earmarked for one thing or another. Most is spent on personal needs or the needs of the family. The risk of failing at a new job, and the resulting hole in the cash flow, is top of mind for many. They simply will not take the risk. I've been there! My fear of losing what I had vs. the potential gains from taking a risk shackled me and kept me from moving forward.

Eventually, I did break the chains. Let me tell you my career story and share a few highlights about the mentors I had.

First there was Clarence. Eight years of production supervision (second and third shift) left me unchallenged. Born out of boredom, I started looking at different ways of doing my job that would lead to improved productivity. I basically kept these ideas to myself. One day, Clarence, my supervisor, caught wind of what I was doing and suggested I schedule some time to review my ideas with him. He felt they could help his entire organization run more smoothly and help him meet his productivity objectives. He created a new job that allowed me to implement these ideas. After a couple of years, Clarence felt I could be more effective if my job was expanded and moved into the Production Scheduling department. My first reaction was fear! What if it didn't work out? What if I screwed up? What if I didn't get along with the new boss? I had no choice. Clarence had faith in me (even though I didn't) and created that very first step in my career path.

And then there was Ray. My experience working in the scheduling area provided many opportunities to learn new skills. A couple of years later, there was an opening in the corporate office (in Ray's group) doing a similar job but on a company-wide scale. It was an easy transition with minimal risk. After three years in Ray's group, we had a chat. He suggested that I was ready to lead a newly created team charged with commercializing the development, manufacture and logistics of new products. Talk about butterflies! Ray gave me the confidence I needed to take the leap and manage the risks (and the rewards) associated with the new job. It turned out to be the best job I ever had. In fact, just about every job since has paled in comparison.

Fast-forward a few years. I was climbing the corporate ladder. With each new job came a little more pay, a few extra stock options and of course, more responsibility. Every few years I would sell the *boss-du jour* on the need to create a new job for me so I could address process gaps. Life was good.

The company underwent a major restructuring that created many new opportunities. I moved from operations, to strategy and eventually to IT.

Then I got a call from Helen. I was *"drafted"* into a new position that would transform the IT function in a fundamental way; a way I really didn't believe in at first. Helen, my first female boss, was fantastic. She knew my strong suit was creative thinking and gave me the freedom to explore and implement ideas. She was great at selling those ideas up-line. We were a great team. The job was challenging and quickly became just as satisfying as the new products job some years earlier.

A few years after I began working for Helen the work world began to change. The organization became more global. Cost reductions drove almost every decision. New jobs were created, the structure changed and people were reporting to new bosses, often in different countries. At the same time, many jobs were eliminated. Then it happened: After 32 years, my job was eliminated. I was crushed, angry and afraid. How could they eliminate my job? What will happen to the team? Who will maintain all that we had created? What will I do?

Then I got a call from Mike. A few weeks after my job was eliminated, I got a call from a mutual acquaintance asking if I would be interested in talking to a company on the West Coast. They desperately needed help managing a project that would transform their IT organization. In many ways it was similar to what I had just left. I hit it off with Mike, the hiring manager, instantly. Our career paths, experiences and core beliefs were very similar as were our management styles. He felt I would be a good fit for his team and convinced me to move to California and take a V.P. job in his group. I had the freedom to pick my team and draft our transition plan.

It was an amazing challenge. The team rose to the occasion and accomplished an extremely difficult transformation on time and within budget. After two years, the time was right for me to move back to the Midwest and consider pursuing my life-long dream of writing. Life is good.

Managing *your* career path.

Everyone has a career path. Some are the result of carefully managed plans. Others grew out of a series of random events. Regardless of how one's career evolved, we can each look back at our job history and clearly see the path leading us to where we are today. Find yourself a good mentor! Many successful people can point to one or more mentors that helped them keep their career moving in a positive direction.

Step 1: Determine what you want to be doing in five to ten years. I'll say it again: identify *what you want to be doing* not the specific job title you want. There is a huge difference. The job is merely a title. What you will be *doing* are the actions and interactions you will perform and/or manage. Once you figure out your goal, identify the skills you will need to achieve it. This is not an easy task but your mentor can help. Did you find one yet?

Step 2: Write down, in sequential order, every job you have held from the very first one, to the job you hold today. This should be a rather simple task.

Step 3: Take a moment and list the motivators and emotions felt when you left one job and took the next. Why did you take the job? How did you feel about it? Motivators might be a promotion; an opportunity to learn new skills; exposure to a different facet of the business; a better working environment or a preferred geographical location. Negative emotions include: fear of the unknown; concerns about being able to perform the job; leaving a comfortable work environment and work friends; being accepted by peers in the new job. Positive emotions include: pride in being recognized for your accomplishments; the opportunity to work in a better environment; prestige and more pay.

Step 4: Highlight the jobs you felt were an essential piece of your career path. These are jobs that taught critical skills; offered unique experiences; or created connections that would generate new opportunities that will lead to your goal.

Step 5: Identify three future jobs that are logical next steps. These jobs may be within or outside of your current organization.

What's the point of these assignments? When you connect the dots between past and future jobs they should, in some way, lead you to your goal. Each successive job should have added something to your skills inventory needed to reach your goal. It is a good idea to share your career aspirations with your immediate manager so that he or she can help identify potential job moves (usually within your current company) that will eventually help get you to your career goal.

Will my manager help me find a different job? I firmly believe that the single most important role for any manager is to coach his or her people on how to achieve their goals. If your goal is to become president of the company, a good manager will never say, "You don't have what it takes to be president." Rather, the manager should offer suggestions about career steps and other opportunities that will add the skills and experiences you will need in order for you to become president.

"When you see a man at the top of a mountain, he didn't fall there!" Each of us can choose to make the sacrifices and do the work necessary to reach our goals. I believe that one's drive is more important than the results. Despite a solid effort, sometimes the mountain wins or events may occur that warrant a change in direction. There is nothing wrong with making career path adjustments along the way. Stay alert to opportunities and take advantage of new options that may come your way.

Jobs are both specific tasks and experiential opportunities.

The various jobs in one's past are specific elements on a path shaping his or her career. As I look back on my own career, it bounced all over the place from a third shift sanitation supervisor in a meat packing plant to vice president at a major fashion retailer. Thinking back, there is no way I could have predicted the end from the events in the beginning.

Stay flexible. It is difficult to create a list of jobs to pursue over a 30-year career. We simply don't know what the workplace will look like that far into the future. Moreover, we don't have any idea about the random opportunities that may happen to come our way.

Rather than focus on specific jobs, first note the experience and skills needed to achieve your career aspirations. Then select jobs that will provide these skills. Your career path planning should be flexible and open to opportunities that will improve your skills and build expertise. The following chart shows a job, its tasks and the transferable skills and experiences it builds.

The Job	Job Tasks	Experiences and Skills
Sanitation Supervisor	• Make sure crews follow procedures • Assure equipment is cleaned before startup	• Managing small teams and meeting deadlines • Working in a large company setting
Production Supervisor	• Train new crew members on their job duties • Manage production and quality standards	• Managing larger teams • Training employees • Working with other functions – QA, IT, etc.
Global Planner	• Set staffing needs at multiple plants • Assure that the right items are produced	• Building relationships with remote locations • Negotiating schedules • International exposure
New Products Manager	• Create processes to manufacture new items • Assure product is on hand for rollout plans • Achieve cost targets	• Project management • Working through issues • Creativity and ideation • Work with other groups • Understand product cost
IT Manager	• Create new programs • Keep systems running • Keep technology current	• Help clients attain goals • Third party experience • Manage large budgets

Reading the signs – is a *"course correction"* needed?

A pendulum never dwells at its center point. It is either moving away from or towards it…until it runs out of energy. The same is true with one's career; it is rarely in steady state. You are either growing your stature or diminishing it. It is important to note that careers will oscillate from hot to not, and back again. You need to be in tune with where you are, especially when you are on the *"not"* side of the equation.

Signs that indicate your career is HOT:

High visibility assignments. Your boss will assign you to lead (or participate on) highly visible projects. These will put you in front of the company's leadership team. Assignments such as these are great opportunities to build your network especially if the project is a success.

Travel opportunities. You are chosen for travel assignments to meet with difficult clients, remote teams, etc. You are encouraged to attend professional conferences in nice places such as San Diego or Las Vegas. Travel is expensive and being chosen for these assignments is a good sign. This is not a time to party. You are representing your company.

Your advice is sought after. When people seek your advice it means you have reached a certain level of expertise in a topic area. More importantly, it may mean you are now regarded as a trusted partner.

Meetings are scheduled around your calendar. This is a sign of power. Your input is regarded as critical and your expertise is important enough to schedule around.

Your office is moved closer to the corner office. Bosses, out of convenience, want to be close to the staff they communicate with frequently. You will know who the rising stars are. They are positioned closer to the boss than others.

Salary and compensation are increasing. When your career is in high gear you will tend to be compensated better than the average for the group you are in. Compensation comes in a variety of ways: salary, stock, perks, etc. I had accepted a position that required significant travel and time away from the family. One of the perks with this job was the use of company-owned vacation homes. In addition to the use of these vacation homes, I was allowed to use accumulated frequent flyer rewards for personal travel. Each year, the family enjoyed these homes and I enjoyed the frequent flier miles to get us there.

Signs that your career is NOT so hot:

Passive-aggressive ostracizing. This technique is used to let a person know that his or her career is in a bad place, without really saying anything directly. You will begin to feel like an *"outsider"* and doubt your value. Even the HR people begin distancing themselves from you. The plan is that you eventually become fed up with the silent treatment and quit.

Communications. You no longer receive *"sensitive"* office communications that you had received in the past. When you ask why you were left off the circulation list you are told it was an oversight. Every time? Come on!

An expert no more! You are no longer the recognized expert in anything. Your input is ignored or pushed aside even though it might be spot on. You are told, *"We will see..."* These are the three most often used words in hell!

Others get the great assignments. You don't get those plumb roles anymore. Your travel to meet with remote teams or attend conferences becomes scrutinized and curtailed.

Your staff is reassigned. An interesting tactic is having your most valued team members reassigned. A couple of them may be chosen to serve on a special *"task force"* reporting directly to your boss. You no longer have the use of their services yet nothing is taken off your plate. You are being set-up to fail. It is time to dust off your resume.

Your office is moved away from the boss. Beware of those that are looking to take your place and your office. They are out there. They will take action when the boss begins to show the slightest signs of disfavor with you. When your office moves away, so should you – to a new employer.

Preparing for your next career move.

Remember this: your career is bigger than the employer and bigger than the job. When your job ends it is time to think rationally not emotionally. Keep yourself ready for the next career move; you never know when one may come along.

Networking. Networking is the single most important activity to help boost your career. To succeed you must continually connect with new people, cultivate new relationships and leverage your network. A network can be invaluable in finding your next job.

Always ask for contacts, rarely a job. For example: *"I'm interested in growing my expertise in (a certain field) and was hoping you might know someone I could connect with to learn more about it."* When you ask for a job, unless there is one available, the answer will be *"No."* This creates an awkward situation for you and the person you asked. Asking for contacts will not create the same level of angst.

Networking is a good way to learn about emerging dynamics within your industry. It is where you can learn about what's new and what's about to change.

Networking creates a ready-list of contacts that will prove invaluable to you someday. It creates a structure to help you search for new opportunities as you build your career.

As your network grows, it naturally leads to more contacts and additional referrals within your industry. Having a well-constructed network of resources not only enhances career development, it provides a potential list of customers for the goods and services your firm produces.

Keep your resume current! It is difficult to whip out a thorough, well written resume on short notice. Invest the time to create a professional looking document. Once created, update it every six months or so. Keep it current, fresh and easily accessible. If you e-mail it, you may want to save and send it as a PDF file. Word docs may look different if the version used to create it is not the same version used to view it. PDF files are more universal and more difficult for someone else to edit.

Non-competes: You should with your HR department to see if you signed any non-compete agreements with your current firm. Your potential employer may ask about them.

What about pursuing a Master's Degree? After ten years in the *"real world"* I decided to pursue my MBA while still working my regular job. The intellectual challenge, the academic atmosphere and the fact that my employer paid for it, all made for an amazing experience. If you are on the fence, I recommend it. It will be a solid step on your journey.

Did the MBA help my career? I believe it did. After earning my MBA I stayed with the employer that paid for it for a number of years. Doors that were shut before the MBA did not magically spring open. However, I had changed. Earning the degree increased my self-confidence and I became more articulate. These qualities, along with the base of experiences I had built, helped my career.

Interestingly, the MBA was more valuable to the firms I interviewed with than it was to the employer that paid for it. It helped leverage a V.P. position at the firm I ultimately moved to. If you have the means, the interest and the time, an investment in education is something that can never be discounted or taken away. Go for it!

Are you willing to make the sacrifice? At some point you will need to make a career decision that impacts others in your life, especially the family. Your next career move may require longer hours, extensive travel and a potential relocation. You need to understand the personal sacrifices and hardships each career change may have on your personal life and the lives of your family. It is best to discuss these before you toss your hat in the ring for that *"plum"* job you have been waiting for. You need to have your family on board and excited about the career change. You cannot be successful without them.

The moment of truth; pursuing a job change.

The phone rings. A headhunter asks if you might know of anyone interested in filling an opening for XYZ Corp. You, of course, are flattered and excited about the prospect of more pay, advancement and better working conditions. Your ego is pumped because someone thinks enough of you to call. The caller is usually an external recruiter hired a firm to conduct a retained search. A retained search means the hiring firm pays their fee if they find a candidate. Sometimes the caller is a recruiter working in the hiring firm's HR department, or may even be a manager within your current company.

The typical recruiter starts the conversation with: "I've been retained to conduct a search for an opening (minimal details) at XYZ Corp. Do you know of anyone with experience and skills that may be interested in this position?"

Keep your cards close to the vest. Avoid the temptation to express your personal interest and don't give the names of others. Nothing good comes from helping the recruiter build a network. In fact, your HR group may have rules against it. You may however, suggest that *you* are, "Interested in learning more about the job, just in case you think of someone that might be a good fit." Be sure to get the recruiter's contact information so you can reach them with a name if/when you find one. At this point it is critical to keep silent. Do not indicate that you are personally interested and do not discuss the call coworkers. Here is what this approach gives you:

1. The details of the job to see if it is a good fit for you.

2. The recruiter's contact information to verify and validate.

3. You remain in control and are under no obligation.

4. You cannot be accused of actively looking for a new job.

Be wary of headhunter calls. Unless you have established a relationship with the caller, you don't know if they are reputable or not. Sometimes (although not common) a firm will conduct fake headhunter calls on their own employees to see who is looking to jump ship. Paranoid managers may try this to test the loyalty of their staff.

If you do have a personal interest in the job, think over the pluses and minuses before pursuing it. Next, do a little research and check out the recruiter's firm. Hiring companies will often use large search firms to create a candidate list to fill key positions. A reputable firm will honor your request for confidentiality. If everything checks out and you want to learn more, contact the recruiter and ask for details about the firm, the job itself, the pay, location, etc. Be sure to update your resume, the recruiter will ask to see it.

Learn as much as you can about the hiring firm. Review recent financial statements (if available) to see if they are solid and solvent or heading for trouble. Are they market leaders or followers? Most importantly, try to learn why the job is open. Is it a newly created position? Did the incumbent leave after many years or only a few months? Etc.

If you decide to pursue the job, you will need more details to finalize your decision. Organize your questions so they focus on two topics: the job itself and the compensation package.

Questions about the job itself:

What are the key aspects of the work and required skills?

What are the major deliverables you will be responsible for?

Where is the job located?

Organization structure and to whom the position will report?

Does the position have staff? If so, how many?

Does the job require travel? If so, what percent of the time?

Questions about the compensation package:

Base salary? Sign-on bonus? Payout agreement?

Annual cash bonus and stock incentive plans?

Who pays for relocation and temporary living expenses?

Pension plans and/or 401 K contributions?

Insurance benefits for Medical, Dental, Life, Disability, etc.?

Vacation policy? How many weeks/days will you get?

Other perks?

Are you ready to take the plunge? You should be able to learn enough from the recruiter to decide if you want to go forward with the next step. To pursue it further, contact the recruiter and request an interview with the hiring firm. They will want to see your resume first. If you have prepared properly you will have an updated version of your resume ready to send. *This is worth repeating:* Save and send your resume as a PDF file. This will help minimize formatting issues that arise when various versions of word processing software are used.

The interview. If you are granted an interview, spend some time doing your homework to learn as much as you can about the firm and its market. This helps you generate intelligent questions to ask during the interview. The first interview may be face-to-face, on the phone, or videoconference. Regardless of the medium used, here are a few *"do's and don'ts"* to keep in mind to make a great first impression.

1. You only get one chance to make a first impression. Ask the recruiter about acceptable office attire. Dress up a bit, be on time and re-read the chapter on body language.

2. Bring a notepad with your questions. It will also come in handy to jot down things discussed during the interview.

3. Listen to the interviewer. Do not interrupt. Answer his or her questions honestly and efficiently. Stay positive and never, ever bad-mouth current or past employers.

4. Explain how your skill and experience will help the firm reach its goals; share past results using data. For example:

    - Managed 100 people with a budget of $10 million and increased productivity by 5% each year. This was accomplished by streamlining cumbersome processes by eliminating bottlenecks.

    - Increased profits by reducing manufacturing costs by 8% ($6 million) over a two-year period. The reduced cost contributed to a 4% increase in sales volume.

    - Restructured IT saving $3,500,000 annually. This was accomplished through a combination of changing the organization structure and strategic outsourcing.

    - Increased output of dealer print ads from 200 per month to over 300. Without adding staff, we focused on making our internal processes more efficient.

5. If you feel the interview is progressing positively it is appropriate to raise the topic of salary and benefits. Don't dwell on this. However, it is important to understand the value of the job in order to decide to pursue it further.

6. When the interview is over, ask the interviewer what the next steps will be. Will they get back to you? If so, when? Should you have further contact with the recruiter?

Post interview. At this point, neither the hiring firm nor you have invested much time or money. If you decide the position is not a good fit for you, end it. Don't drag it on wasting your time or that of the recruiter and the firm. Continuing the process only to refuse a valid job offer, casts a very dark shadow on you. After the first interview, you will know enough about the job to make a *"go"* or *"no-go"* decision.

Be sure to send the interviewer a brief note of thanks for the time spent talking with you. If you want to pursue the job further, express your interest and desire for follow-up. Ask any additional questions you may have in this note. Example:

> *Thank you so much for the opportunity to interview with you for the teaching position at East Seguardo. I enjoyed learning about the position and I am very excited about this potential opportunity.*
>
> *If offered the opportunity to be part of the East Sequardo team, I assure you my abilities in differentiation, classroom management, problem solving, and collaboration would be an asset to the students, parents, and staff.*
>
> *Thank you again for interviewing me. I look forward to the opportunity to join the East Seguardo staff and look forward to hearing from you soon.*

What you say can (an will) be used against you! If the job will create a change to your home life (travel, more hours, etc.) you should discuss it with your spouse. If you have a trusted confidant or mentor outside of the workplace, you may find it beneficial to walk through the alternatives with that person too. However, I wouldn't broadcast anything to your friends, relatives, co-workers, etc. Gossip is amazingly efficient.

Your ego is sky-high because another firm has expressed an interest in your skills and capabilities. That's understandable, but sharing this with anyone in your workplace will get back to the boss and that's not good. The only outcome of telling anyone is that it fuels your ego. Unfortunately, fueling the ego doesn't improve your chances of getting the job, and it may destroy the relationship with your current boss.

If your interview went well, you will really be pumped and excited; but a good interview is not a solid job offer! Telling people about the job before you have officially been offered and accepted it will create issues and expectations:

People will assume you are actually getting the job or you wouldn't be talking about it. If, for some reason, you don't get it they will wonder what *you* did to blow it!

As your co-workers begin to anticipate your departure, they will start eyeing-up your stuff (the desk, office art, etc.).

Nothing good comes from telling anyone about the interview. My advice is to maintain silence for now.

Evaluating and negotiating the job offer: Assuming you did a great job impressing the first interviewer, some additional interviews may be arranged before the firm is ready to make an offer. Firms will want to meet with you face-to-face. If travel is required for further interviews, it is customary for the hiring firm to reimburse you for the cost. Be sure to discuss travel details with the interviewer or the firm's HR person. Be clear about the date and time as well as your role in making travel arrangements. For example, will you need to schedule your own flight and reserve a hotel room or will they do this for you? Larger firms use their own internal travel department to save money on airfare and hotels. As you progress through the interview process, the hiring firm may invite you to bring your spouse along for a visit too.

Congratulations! You have successfully made it through the interview gauntlet and the firm offers you the job. A job offer, until accepted, might be open to some negotiating. Be sure to ask for a couple of days to evaluate the total package being offered (most firms will be fine with this). Be sure to get all the details and don't bite at it yet. You want the job so bad you can taste it, but don't say, *"yes"* quite yet. Keep in mind the firm offered you the job. They want you. If you remember anything from this book, remember this: Once you accept the job, all negotiating stops! If there are things you want (more money, a car, paid housing, a certain title, stock options, 401K, vacation time, relocation assistance, etc.) the time to ask is before you formally accept the offer, not after. Don't be surprised if they don't give you everything you ask for, so keep your list of wants and needs realistic.

Get it in writing. Once you and the new firm agree on terms, ask them to send you a note clarifying everything that was agreed to. This will assure that both parties are on the same page. Before you formally accept the job, give it one more mental review. Discuss the details with your mentor and spouse to assure he or she is 100% behind you. Make sure you are committed before you accept it.

Upon acceptance, you can discuss the start date, matriculation process (i.e. training, setting up an internet id, transferring your 401K, etc.) and the relocation process. Large firms may have an in-house relocation team to make your move easier.

Breaking the news to your old boss: You should let your old boss know you have decided to leave. Do this as close to the start date with the new company as possible. Two weeks notice is customary. Keep in mind that many things may impact the hiring firm's plans. Mergers, acquisitions, recessions, new management, etc. may force the hiring firm to rescind their offer. Few things are as awkward as announcing you are leaving and then asking for you old job back. Also, if you tell your boss you are leaving in two months, you might be axed in two weeks. You may not want to be without income for that long. Once again I urge you to resist the desire to discuss the job change with co-workers and friends and for crying out loud, keep it off the social media sites. Always ask, "What good comes from telling anyone?"

If you feel obligated to tell every detail, don't. You are not required to tell the old employer anything other than the last day you will be in the office. You don't need to explain why you are leaving; the details of your new job; who the new employer is; or the new salary. The less said, the better.

Be prepared for a counter offer. Your old company may have policies that prevent negotiating with someone who quits. Then again, it may be the case that your old firm authorizes your soon-to-be x-boss to approach you with a counter-offer. They may try to talk you into staying by offering a better position and more money than the new firm offered. Try not to cave in. If they really thought that highly of you they would have done something long before you got fed up and decided to look elsewhere. Avoid the temptation to get into a bidding war. Nothing damages your reputation as fast as accepting the new job and then having second thoughts.

Those reasons for deciding to leave in the first place will still be present and more money won't change them. Naturally, you will be flattered to be the booty in this catfight. Remember that talk is cheap and much of what is promised by your current company may never come to fruition.

If they offer the moon (and you are considering turning tail on the new firm) ask that the terms be put in writing, noting specifics about dollars, dates, details, etc. Insist that an officer of the firm (VP level or higher) and someone from HR sign it. Don't even think about considering this counter offer without those signatures.

Once your path is set and all the discussion is final, your old boss, if a professional, will wish you well and thank you for your service. It is not customary to have a company hosted going away party. If anything, you may want to invite a few of your close friends from the office to join you for beer after work on your last day. You should pick up the check; you are the one that just got a raise!

Stay professional. What you need to do is act in a professional manner and resist the urge to burn your bridges. You may need a reference some day and who knows, you may cross paths in the future. Try to maintain a cordial relationship to keep the doors open for future opportunities. Leaving on good terms makes future associations easier to navigate.

The first day with the new employer. Your career cycle has just turned a full revolution. You are a new hire once again, albeit with a bit more experience than last time. You need to learn the many nuances of the new workplace and how to survive and thrive in it. It may be a good idea to re-read this book from the beginning. It made a difference the first time!

In Closing . . .

I hope you have enjoyed reading *Winning in the Workplace* as much as I enjoyed writing it. My intent with this book was to provide suggestions to those wishing to develop the *soft skills* necessary to not only survive, but to thrive in the workplace. The book is based in large part on my personal experiences.

For many of people, their job is something they *have* to do in order to have the money to do the things they *want* to do! Nothing more. For these folks, developing a career is not part of their psyche. Their job is simply the means to an end, not the end in itself. They give an honest day's work for an honest day's pay. In time, they may be promoted to higher levels of pay and responsibility. At the end of the day, they are able to disengage from the job and focus their free time on family and friends.

For others, their career *is* the end…period! These people are driven. They work long hours perfecting their craft. Often working hand-to-mouth, they will sacrifice a great deal for the sake of their career. Some will eventually make it to the top of their pyramid. A great many more will enjoy the ride for as far as it will carry them.

Still others will approach work and life with balance in mind. They recognize that developing their career is an important piece of their lives. They will work hard and make sacrifices to further their careers. At the same time they are able to balance their home-life priorities too. They are committed to their careers and will do whatever it takes to get the job done properly. However, their personal philosophy is *family first*.

Which type are you? Once you figure that out you will be able to make career decisions and choose employers that offer the resources and opportunities to appropriately accommodate your needs.

Best wishes!

www.ingramcontent.com/pod-product-compliance
Lightning Source LLC
LaVergne TN
LVHW051604070426
835507LV00021B/2764